Eat and Explore
Arkansas

Eat and Explore
Arkansas

Great American Publishers
www.GreatAmericanPublishers.com

toll-free 1.888.854.5954

Great American Publishers

P.O. Box 1305 • Kosciusko, MS 39090

toll-free 1.888.854.5954 • www.GreatAmericanPublishers.com

ISBN 978-1-934817-09-4 (1-934817-09-0)

First Edition
10 9 8 7 6 5 4 3 2 1

by Christy Campbell

Layout and design by Lacy Fikes

Front Cover Image, Mark P. Anderson, Big Whiskey Design Studio
Back cover festival image, Magnolia Blossom Festival
Back cover food image, Lacy Fikes Photography © Great American Publishers
Chapter opening photos, istockphoto.com: Appetizers & Beverages p9 © Smokingdrum
Soups Salads & Breads p41 © funwithfood • Vegetables & Other Side Dishes p71
© Diana Didyk • Meat & Seafood p105 © Ezhicheg • Desserts & Other Sweets p137
© Edward ONeil Photography • Index p171 © 2nd Look Graphics

Contents

Introduction

Arkansas has had several nicknames throughout its history, and I do believe they have a winner with "The Natural State." When I began this journey, my knowledge of Arkansas was very limited. In the past I had visited Eureka Springs, done business in Bentonville, and accompanied my husband to Little Rock. It wasn't until I began learning of Arkansas' magnificent lakes and mountains, its miles and miles of trails, the crystals and diamonds, and regional crops – the abundance of grapes, rice, strawberries, tomatoes, sorghum – that I knew I had truly discovered a hidden gem within the vastness of the United States.

In addition to Arkansas' plentiful natural resources, it was a pleasure to discover its traditions. Festivals that have celebrated for decades and the committed communities that support them are part of a heritage that spans generations. I discovered an array of diversity within the culture of Arkansas: a homestead depicting a simpler time, a parade for German cars only, a giant statue of Christianity's central figure, majestic architectural styles from around the globe, and a gathering in honor of toads are just a small sampling of the unique customs and ways of life tucked into every nook and cranny throughout the state.

Then there's the food... our publisher and my personal mentor, Sheila Simmons, can always tell how good a cookbook is by how often she wants to stop reading and start cooking. And that is exactly what she said while viewing the rough draft of this cookbook. As varied as the culture, thus is the food. There are tried and true Southern favorites like *My Favorite Garden Potato Salad* and *Sweet Potato Casserole*, but it doesn't stop with quintessential Southern fare. *Lavender Chocolate Fudge*, *Cherry Coke Salad*, and *Roasted Zucchini with Ricotta and Mint* are culinary delights for cooks of all types. Of course, *Dorothy's Mile High Strawberry Pie*, *Veggie Chicken Wraps*, and *Gourmet Meatloaf* are favorites I am always happy to see at the dinner table.

Every great journey of discovery should be shared to be truly appreciated, and I could not have completed this one without the outstanding team at Great American Publishers and the good people of Arkansas. Brooke Craig, Anita Musgrove, Krista Griffin, Serena Neal, Courtney Rust – thank all of you so much for taking me in and making me welcome. As we kicked into gear, the Arkansas Department of Tourism helped steer us in the right direction, and I appreciate Donna Perrin for understanding our quest right from the beginning.

As it had to be shared, this project also needed someone to 'man the map' and it could not have been done without the right arm of all things Eat & Explore, Christy Jenkins. Christy turned over every leaf in Arkansas to find the pulse of this wonderful part of America, and I am thankful to have her as a tour guide. Roger Simmons' input proved invaluable, right up to the very end. A very special thank you goes to Lacy Fikes, the designer and photographer who was literally dropped in our laps from the heavens. And none of it would be possible without Sheila Simmons, a person whose experience, kindness, and knowledge of all things under the sun continues to motivate and inspire, year after year. To Michael, Michael-Jason, and Preston, your love, support, and patience is the biggest deal of all – thank you.

Eat & Explore Arkansas is not only a journey through the kitchens, celebrations and history of the Natural State, it is the beginning of a larger mission. It is the starting point of our quest to preserve America's traditions, the food we share and the experiences that define us... I look forward to bumping into you again in the future, in another stopping place in the road. Until then, have fun exploring... Arkansas.

Christy Campbell

Appetizers & Beverages

Perfect Party Mix

3 cups Rice Chex
3 cups Corn Chex
3 cups Cheerios
3 cups pretzel sticks
2 cups dry roasted peanuts
1 (12-ounce) package M&M's candy
1 (16-ounce) package white chocolate

Combine cereals, pretzel sticks, peanuts and M&M's in a large bowl. In microwave, melt white chocolate and slowly pour over dry mixture while still warm. Mix to coat evenly. Spread mixture on wax paper and let stand until cool. Break into bite-size pieces. Store in air-tight container in refrigerator to keep fresh.

Quadrangle Festival

Quadrangle Festival
Early October

Downtown Texarkana
903.793.4831
www.texarkanamuseums.org

For over 25 years, artists, craftsmen, and musicians from across the United States have come to Texarkana for the Quadrangle Festival. Voted 'Best Festival' for four years running, the Quadrangle Festival will light up the streets year after year.

The main attraction is the music, so bring your dancin' shoes and get ready to get down. Texarkana hosts two nights of concerts and street dances with some of the best names in music. But that's not all. Annual events include a barbecue cook-off, the children's talent search, and the ever popular Battle of the Bands. Who knows? Maybe you and your friends will be lucky enough to cheer for the next big name in music...

All proceeds from the Quadrangle Festival benefit the Texarkana Museums Systems. Call 903.793.4831 or visit www.texarkanamuseums.org to find out more about dates and admission.

Ozark Trail Granola

3 cups rolled oats
1 cup sliced almonds
¼ cup brown sugar
½ teaspoon cinnamon
½ teaspoon nutmeg
⅓ cup vegetable oil
⅓ cup maple syrup or honey
1 teaspoon vanilla
½ cup raisins

Preheat oven to 300°. Combine oats, almonds, raisins, brown sugar, cinnamon and nutmeg in a large bowl. Mix well. In a separate bowl combine oil, syrup and vanilla. Stir well and add to the dry mixture, tossing until well coated. Spread the mixture on a cookie sheet and bake 30 minutes, turning over every 5 minutes. Remove from oven to cool, but leave in cookie sheet. After completely cool, stir in raisins and store in an airtight container. Put some in a Ziploc bag and hit the trail.

Ace of Clubs House and Museum

420 Pine Street • Texarkana

Have you ever visited a house built in the shape of the ace of clubs from a deck of playing cards? When traveling through Texarkana, be sure to stop at the Ace of Clubs House and Museum and cross it off your list. According to legend, the house was built with winnings from a poker game. It is truly one of the most unique and beautiful museum homes in America.

Roasted Almonds

1 tablespoon chili powder
1 tablespoon extra-virgin olive oil
½ teaspoon salt
½ teaspoon ground cumin
½ teaspoon ground coriander
¼ teaspoon ground cinnamon
¼ teaspoon black pepper
2 cups whole almonds

Preheat oven to 350°. In a medium bowl, combine chili powder, oil, salt, cumin, coriander, cinnamon and pepper. Toss in almonds and coat thoroughly. Place in a 9x13-inch pan. Bake 10 minutes or until almonds are toasted, stirring twice. Cool almonds completely before serving. This will keep in an airtight container for 4 days.

Seasoned Snack Crackers

½ teaspoon lemon pepper
½ teaspoon dill weed
1 (1-ounce) package dry ranch dressing mix
1 teaspoon garlic powder
¾ cup oil
1 (12-ounce) bag oyster crackers

Mix together lemon pepper, dill weed, dry ranch mix, garlic powder and oil. Pour over oyster crackers and stir.

Mt. Magazine International Butterfly Festival

Delicious Ham Spread

2 cups high-quality ham,
    chopped into very small pieces
½ cup mayonnaise
2 hard-boiled eggs, chopped very small
½ cup sweet pickle relish
2 tablespoons chopped onion
Dash ground cloves

Combine all ingredients in a bowl. Mix well and chill. Serve with party rye bread.

Just Right Cheese Ring

I have used different types of preserves for this: raspberry, blackberry, plum...
Be creative and use what suits your taste.

2 cups shredded Cheddar cheese
1 cup chopped pecans
¾ cup mayonnaise
1 medium onion, chopped very fine
1 clove garlic, minced
½ teaspoon Tabasco
1 cup strawberry preserves

Mix first 6 ingredients and form into a ring. Cover and chill about 2 hours. Fill center with strawberry preserves and serve with your favorite crackers.

Appetizing Apricot Cheese Ball

2 (8-ounce) packages cream cheese, softened
½ cup chopped green onions
1 small package real bacon bits
2 tablespoons apricot preserves
½ cup chopped pecans

Combine first 4 ingredients and shape into a ball. Roll cheese ball mixture in chopped pecans. Chill for 2 hours or more.

Tour da' Delta

Game Day Cheese Ball

2 cups grated Cheddar cheese
1 teaspoon Worcestershire sauce
1 (3-ounce) package cream cheese
Dash red pepper
1 tablespoon minced onion
2 teaspoons lemon juice
½ cup chopped pecans

Combine all ingredients except pecans. Shape into a ball. Roll in chopped pecans. Serve with crackers.

Wine Country Cottage

523 Baxter Street • Altus
479.209.2367 • www.arwinecountrycottage.com

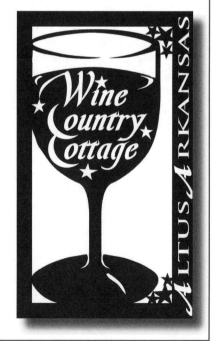

Are you ready for a relaxing stay while you tour Arkansas wine country? Then the Wine Country Cottage is the place for you. Located in Altus, Arkansas, the Wine Country Cottage is a 3 bedroom, 1½ bath, fully furnished cottage featuring all the amenities of home. The spacious front deck is perfect for sitting and enjoying the beautiful Arkansas weather and the back deck is ideal for a summer gathering and is equipped with a barbecue grill. The wine-themed bedrooms offer a luxurious place to rest, and the Tuscan-themed dining area will transport you to a time and place far removed from the hectic schedule of daily life. The Wine Country Cottage is located within walking distance of many local attractions. After walking to the Heritage House Museum, or strolling through the beautiful City Park, it's time to jump in the car for a short ride to the many wineries that offer juice and wine tasting and winery/vineyard tours. The Wine Country Cottage is the perfect home away from home that you're looking for. Call 479.209.2367 to book it today.... Your Cottage escape awaits!

Best Benedictine in all of Arkansas

1 cucumber, peeled and seeded
1 small sweet onion
4 (8-ounce) packages cream cheese, softened
½ cup sour cream
½ cup mayonnaise
Salt to taste
1 or 2 drops green food coloring

Mix cucumber and onion in a food processor. Combine cumber mixture with cream cheese in a large bowl. Stir in sour cream and mayonnaise; add salt to taste. Drop green food coloring, adding enough to make a light green color. Serve as a dip with your favorite chips or crackers, or use as a sandwich spread.

Purplehull Pea Fritters

1 cup fresh shelled purplehull peas
1 egg, beaten
½ cup finely chopped onion
1 teaspoon salt
¼ teaspoon ground red pepper
Vegetable oil

If the peas are not very tender and young, simmer them in boiling water for 10 to 15 minutes first. Process peas in blender or food processor. Combine well with egg, onion, salt, and ground red pepper. In a heavy frying pan, heat oil to 375°, or until smoky haze appears. Drop mixture by teaspoonfuls into the hot oil and fry until golden brown on both sides. Drain on paper towels. Serve hot as an accompaniment to cocktails or as an appetizer. Makes 4 to 6 servings.

Purplehull Pea Festival
& World Championship Rotary Tiller Race

Smackover Roughneck Dip

6 to 7 jalapeños
1 tablespoon lemon juice
½ cup vegetable oil
1 quart mayonnaise
2 cans tomato paste
1 tablespoon garlic powder
2 tablespoons prepared mustard

Cut ends from jalapeños, slice lengthwise and remove seeds. Combine in blender with lemon juice and vegetable oil; process until smooth. Set aside. Combine mayonnaise, tomato paste, garlic powder, and mustard. Just before serving, mix with jalapeño mixture and serve with chips.

Oil Town Festival

Oil Town Festival
Third Weekend in June

City Park Broadway & 10th
Smackover
870.944.0221/870.725.3521
www.smackoverar.com

If you are looking for somewhere to be the third weekend in June, then the Oil Town Festival and Duck Race should be on the radar. You can find it in Tennyson Park at 10th and Broadway in Smackover. Let the games begin! The Yellow Duck Race is the biggest draw. Each year 3000 yellow ducks attempt to claim the $1000 first place prize. Don't have a duck to race? No worries, the festival has 17 different contests including watermelon eating and turtle races. There are 5 tournaments including arm wrestling, 3 on 3 basketball, and the bass tournament. The Oil Town Festival is proud to boast the oldest 5K run in the state. And it doesn't stop there. Horseshoe pitching, a bench press contest, a rib cook-off, a bake off, a dog contest, egg toss, a kid's corner with water slides and a rock climbing wall are all part of the festivities. Wind down from the competitions with live music each and every night. Most of the events are free of charge. Now that's a value that can't be beat!

PurpleHull Pea Dip

4 cups purplehull peas, cooked and drained
5 jalapeño peppers (from a jar)
1 tablespoon jalapeño juice
½ medium onion, chopped
1 (4-ounce) can green chilies
1 clove garlic
½ pound Old English sharp cheese
¼ pound (1 stick) butter

Mix purplehull peas, jalapeño peppers and juice, onions, chilies and garlic in blender. Work with ½ to ¼ at a time if load is too much for blender. Heat cheese and butter in double boiler until melted. Stir in pea mixture. Serve in chafing dish with chips.

Note: Adjust peppers and chilies measurement to personal taste.

PurpleHull Pea Festival
& World Championship Rotary Tiller Race

Crawfish Party Dip

A family favorite for special occasions!

1 pound domestic crawfish tail meat, rinsed and drained
1 tablespoon butter
1 heaping teaspoon plus ½ teaspoon
   Delta Donnie's Cajun Sprinkle, divided
2 (8-ounce) packages cream cheese, at room temperature
1 bell pepper, diced
1 small red onion, diced
2 cups cocktail sauce
½ cup finely chopped green onions

Sauté tail meat in a pan with 1 tablespoon butter for 2 minutes. Season with ½ teaspoon Delta Donnie's Cajun Sprinkle. Set aside to cool completely. Mix cream cheese, bell pepper, red onion and 1 heaping teaspoon Delta Donnie's Cajun Sprinkle in a bowl. Spread onto a serving tray evenly about ¾ inch deep. Spread cocktail sauce over top of cream cheese mixture. Sprinkle crawfish tails and green onions on top of that. Serve with crackers and or vegetable sticks.

Delta Crawfish Market & Cafe

Everyone's Favorite Chipped Beef Dip

2 (8-ounce) packages cream cheese, softened
1 (10-ounce) can Rotel (tomatoes & green chilies)
1 bunch green onions, chopped
1 (2-ounce) jar dried beef, chopped

Mix cream cheese with tomatoes. Stir in onions. Add dried beef and mix well. Chill until serving time. Serve with chips or crackers.

Eloise Oliver
BPW Barn Sale

BPW Barn Sale
Last Saturday in September

**The Historic Tate Barn
Camden
870.231.6244
www.bpwbarnsale.org**

In 1968, Ms. Ruth Tate and the Camden Business and Professional Women's Association needed a way to raise funds for a nursing scholarship. A flea market was held, and little did they know that from this humble beginning would grow the largest arts and crafts show in South Arkansas.

The historic Tate Barn is the site for this fun-filled annual event. Under the shade of beautiful oak trees you will discover 100% handmade crafts from 160 different artisans from throughout the South. As you stroll throughout the grounds, the sounds of live music and the aroma of delicious food will fill the air. In addition to music, food and original creations, you will find activities for children, a 5K run for the local athletes, and the Antique and Classic Car Show. There is something for everyone at the BPW Barn Sale, and once family and friends attend once they will comea again, year after year.

Hot Artichoke Dip

2 (14-ounce) cans artichoke hearts,
    drained and chopped
1 cup mayonnaise
¾ cup Parmesan cheese
½ package Italian salad dressing mix
1 cup grated Swiss cheese
¼ cup grated mozzarella cheese

Preheat oven to 350°. Combine all ingredients except the mozzarella cheese and place in a medium casserole dish. Top with mozzarella cheese and bake 25 to 30 minutes or until brown and bubbly. Serve with tortilla chips or wheat thins.

Hot Corn Dip

2 cans shoe peg corn, drained
1 (8-ounce) package cream cheese
2 cans Rotel tomatoes, drained
2 tablespoons jalapeño, chopped
½ teaspoon cumin
¼ teaspoon garlic
½ teaspoon chili powder

Mix well and heat in a microwave or oven. Serve with corn chips.

Cammie Hambrice
Magnolia Chamber of Commerce
Magnolia Blossom Festival & World Championship Steak Cook-Off®

Colorful Corn Dip

1 small jar Pace picante sauce
1 cup mayonnaise
2 cups shredded Cheddar cheese
2 cans Mexicorn
6 green onions, chopped

Mix picante sauce, mayonnaise, cheese, corn and onions. Store in airtight container and chill well before serving. Goes with any good dipping chip.

Confetti Dip

8 ounces Monterey Jack cheese, shredded
1 (4-ounce) can chopped green chiles
I (4-ounce) can chopped black olives
4 green onions, chopped
1 tomato, chopped
¼ cup minced fresh cilantro
½ cup Italian salad dressing

Combine cheese, green chiles, black olives, green onions, tomato, cilantro and salad dressing in a bowl and mix well. Chill, covered, 8 to 12 hours. Serve with tortilla chips.

Note: *This recipe may be doubled. You may substitute shredded Colby/Monterey Jack cheese.*

Junior League of Pine Bluff
Pine Bluff Convention and Visitors Bureau

Maggie's Phenomenal Dip

1 (8-ounce) package cream cheese, softened
1 cup mayonnaise
1 cup grated Swiss cheese
1 bunch green onions, chopped
½ cup cooked and crumbled bacon
½ cup crumbled Ritz crackers,
    plus more for serving

Mix cream cheese, mayonnaise, Swiss and onions. Spread in 8x8-inch pan.
Top with crumbled bacon and Ritz crackers. Bake at 350° for 20 to 30 minutes.
Serve with Ritz crackers for dipping or spreading.

Bella Vista Arts & Crafts Festival

Bella Vista Arts & Crafts Festival
Third Weekend in October

Bella Vista
479.855.2064
www.bellavistafestival.org

For this world-renowned arts and crafts weekend in October, Northwest Arkansas is awash with some 200,000 visitors from across the country. The Bella Vista Arts & Crafts Festival has celebrated over 42 years and is now the PREMIER show in all Arkansas. The Festival is sponsored by the non-profit Village Art Club. Profits from the Festival provide scholarships for promising artists, continuing education for artists and artisans, and go toward the support of the artisan co-op Wishing Spring Gallery. Over 300 booths provide visitors with the finest art pieces and the finest craft items that are available—always hand-made! Come browse our beautiful, tree surrounded grounds while you find that special gift for someone—or yourself! We have free parking and free transportation to and from the parking areas and you can enjoy a full day of delicious meals from our unique and diverse food providers. Located on the beautiful grounds close to Hwy 279 (Forest Hills Blvd) and Hwy 340 (Lancashire) in Bella Vista, Arkansas. (For GPS the address is 1991 Forest Hills Blvd)

Green Olive Dip

2 (8-ounce) packages cream cheese, softened
½ cup Miracle Whip
½ cup (2 ounces) chopped pecans
1 cup (7-ounce jar) green olives, chopped
2 tablespoons olive juice
Dash pepper (no salt)

Mix well and refrigerate overnight. Serve with corn chips or as a spread for finger sandwiches.

Cammie Hambrice
Magnolia Chamber of Commerce
Magnolia Blossom Festival & World Championship Steak Cook-Off®

Black Bean Salsa

2 (15-ounce) cans black beans, rinsed and drained
1 (17-ounce) can whole-kernel corn, drained
2 large ripe tomatoes, seeded and chopped
1 large ripe Haas avocado, peeled and chopped
1 jalapeño, seeded and chopped
1 red onion, chopped
¼ cup chopped cilantro
4 tablespoons fresh lime juice
2 tablespoons olive oil
1 tablespoon red wine vinegar
1 teaspoon salt
½ teaspoon freshly ground black pepper

Combine all ingredients in a large bowl. Cover and chill. Serve with tortilla chips.

Pear Honey

14 medium pears, peeled and cored
8 cups sugar
1 (20-ounce) can crushed pineapple, undrained
3 tablespoons lemon juice

Grind pears a little in food processor. Mix all ingredients together in a large kettle and bring to a boil. Reduce heat; cook and stir uncovered about 50 minutes. Remove from heat; pour in hot jars, adjust caps. Process 20 minutes in boiling water bath. Makes 6 pints. Very good!!

Emillie Jackson
Diamond City Festival

Fruit Dip

1 jar marshmallow cream
1 (8-ounce) package cream cheese, softened
1 (8-ounce) carton sour cream
1 can sweetened condensed milk

Combine all ingredients in electric blender. Beat until smooth, scraping sides if needed. Chill at least 1 hour. Serve with assorted fruit.

Creamy Pumpkin Dip

2 (8-ounce) packages cream cheese, softened
1 (16-ounce) box powdered sugar
1 (16-ounce) can pumpkin
2 teaspoons ground cinnamon
½ teaspoon ground nutmeg

Beat cream cheese at medium speed until creamy. Gradually add sugar. Beat well. Stir in pumpkin, cinnamon and nutmeg. Serve immediately or cover and chill. Serve with gingersnaps for dipping.

Hot Springs Arts & Crafts Fair

Cream Cheese Stuffed Mushrooms

1 pound bacon
1 bunch green onions, chopped
2 cloves garlic, minced
1 (8-ounce) package cream cheese, cubed
1 cup grated Parmesan cheese
2 large containers mushrooms, stems removed

Fry, drain and crumble bacon. Add chopped green onions and minced garlic at the end of frying. Add cream cheese and Parmesan cheese. Combine thoroughly until cream cheese is melted. Place mushrooms upside down on baking sheet and stuff with mixture. Bake at 350° for 15 to 20 minutes.

Bathhouse Row

Take a stroll down the Grande Promenade and visit many historic bathhouses on Bathhouse Row in Hot Springs. In the late 19th and early 20th centuries, the hot springs were sought by people from around the globe to treat a variety of medical ailments. As medical advances progressed, the hot springs popularity declined. Today, Bathhouse Row is the centerpiece for Hot Springs National Park, and the visitor center is located in The Fordyce. Displaying a wonderful variety of architectural styles from Neoclassical Revival, Renaissance Revival, Spanish and Italianate, it is the largest grouping of its kind in North America.

Delta Poppers

Served as an entree, appetizer, and on po-boys at the Cajun Cafe.

1 teaspoon Delta Donnie's Cajun Sprinkle
1 cup all-purpose flour
1 egg, beaten
1 pound domestic crawfish tail meat

Mix Cajun Sprinkle into flour. In a separate bowl, fold egg into crawfish tail meat to coat evenly. Fold tail meat into seasoned flour and mix until separated, adding more flour if necessary. Deep fry at 350° to 375° until golden brown (about 90 seconds). Drain and serve on lettuce leaf with rémoulade or cocktail sauce.

Delta Crawfish Market & Cafe

Smokin' Pepper Poppers

1 (8-ounce) package cream cheese, softened
1 cup grated sharp Cheddar cheese
1 cup grated Monterey Jack cheese
6 bacon slices, cooked and crumbled
¼ teaspoon salt
¼ teaspoon chili powder
¼ teaspoon garlic powder
1 pound fresh jalapeño peppers,
    halved lengthwise and seeded
½ cup breadcrumbs

Preheat oven to 350°. Combine cream cheese, Cheddar cheese, Monterey Jack cheese, bacon, salt, chili powder, and garlic powder. Spoon 2 tablespoons into each pepper half and shape them. Roll in breadcrumbs. Place in a greased 9x13-inch pan. Bake, uncovered, 20 minutes for smoking hot, 30 minutes for medium, and 40 minutes for mild. Serve hot with ranch dip on the side.

Perfect-for-the-Party Chicken

½ cup margarine
½ cup soy sauce
½ cup red wine
¼ cup lemon juice
1 cup firmly packed brown sugar
2 teaspoons dry mustard
½ teaspoon minced garlic
Black pepper to taste
30 to 45 chicken wings, cut at the joint

Combine margarine, soy sauce, red wine, lemon juice, brown sugar, mustard, garlic and black pepper in saucepan over medium heat. Heat until brown sugar is dissolved, stirring constantly. Place chicken in 9x13-inch baking dish. Pour warm sauce over chicken and let stand 45 minutes. Preheat oven to 350°, place chicken in oven, and then reduce temperature to 250°. Bake 4 to 5 hours, turning wings several times. During final 30 minutes, drain off any excess sauce and return wings to oven, allowing them to slightly brown.

Mother's Best Music Fest

Mother's Best Music Fest
Every Summer in June

Delta Cultural Center
Helena
800.358.0972
www.deltaculturalcenter.com

Every summer, music fans travel from around the world to walk the streets of Helena because of its roots to all forms of music. The Delta Cultural Center presents the Delta Family Gospel Festival and Mother's Best Music Fest. Each festival is a celebration of the diversity of music created throughout the Delta. A variety of music is performed, from blues to rockabilly, country, and Americana sounds. There is no cost for admission, everyone is encouraged to come downtown and enjoy live, original music from musical artist of all types. The music begins at mid-morning and goes until the evening.

Blue Cheese Roast Beef Bites

½ cup butter, softened
2 cups crumbled blue cheese
¼ cup cooked and crumbled bacon
6 slices dark rye bread
6 slices Swiss cheese
6 slices deli roast beef
6 thin slices red onion
Sliced dill pickles

In a small bowl, beat butter and blue cheese until smooth. Mix in bacon. Spread cheese mixture evenly on each slice of bread. Top with Swiss cheese (cut to the same size as the bread). Place on baking sheet and broil until cheese is melted, about 1 minute. Top each with roast beef, onion and pickle. Using a serrated edge knife, cut each in fourths for bite-sized open faced sandwiches.

Crater of Diamonds State Park

They say diamonds are a girls best friends, but digging for diamonds appeals to men and women alike. The Crater of Diamonds State Park is home to the world's only diamond mine open to the public. Visitors are invited to search in the park's diamond search area. 95 million years ago a volcano pipe brought to the surface amazing diamonds and other semi-precious stones. What a wonderful way to spend a vacation—with family, friends, and diamonds!

Party Rounds

2 loaves thin-sliced white bread
½ cup margarine plus more for spreading, softened
2 (8-ounce) packages cream cheese, softened
⅓ cup mayonnaise
6 green onions, chopped
Grated Parmesan cheese for topping

Remove crust from bread and divide each slice into 4 square pieces. Butter one side of each square and place in one layer, butter side up, on baking sheet. Broil until lightly toasted, then turn and lightly toast unbuttered side. Combine cream cheese, ½ cup margarine, mayonnaise, and green onions. Spoon 1 teaspoon cream cheese mixture on buttered sides of toast and top with Parmesan cheese. Place in oven and lightly broil until bubbly and golden, about 5 minutes. Serve warm.

Mozzarella Wedges

1 (8-ounce) tube refrigerated crescent rolls
1 tablespoon butter, melted
¼ teaspoon garlic powder, more to taste
2 cups shredded mozzarella cheese

Preheat oven to 375°. Roll out crescent rolls into a pizza pan. Press flat and to the edge of the pan, sealing perforations. Brush with butter; sprinkle with garlic powder and cheese. Bake 15 to 17 minutes or until crust is golden brown and cheese is lightly browned. Cut into small wedges and serve warm.

Snack Olives

2 cups flour
8 ounces (2 cups) grated cheese
½ cup melted butter
1 jar Spanish olives (at least 36)

Mix flour, cheese and butter into a dough. Cover each olive with about 1 tablespoon of the pastry. Place on an ungreased cookie sheet. Refrigerate 1 hour. Bake at 400° for 15 to 20 minutes.

Wildflower Bed & Breakfast On the Square

Perfect Picnic Celery

1 (8-ounce) package cream cheese, softened
¼ cup mayonnaise
1 jar pimentos, drained
¼ cup chopped green olives
¼ cup chopped nuts, optional
4 stalks celery, washed and scraped
Paprika to taste

Combine cream cheese, mayonnaise, pimentos, olives and nuts. Fill hollows of celery with mixture and smooth off with a knife. Chill several hours. Before serving, sprinkle with paprika and cut into 1½ thick slices. Stick with a toothpick and serve.

The Square in Mountain View

The Historic Downtown Square in Mountain View is famous for its informal musical gatherings, or "pickings," that take place on the lawn around the county courthouse. Bring a chair, kick back, and enjoy the music. While you're there, make time for shopping. The Square is home to unique craft, gift, and antique shops. And when your shopping is done, stop and refuel in the restaurants and snack bars scattered around the square.

Tostada Bites

1½ cups cooked black beans
1 large clove garlic, minced
2 ripe plum tomatoes,
    seeded and cut into ½ inch cubes
Zest of 1 lime
3 tablespoons fresh lime juice, divided
3 tablespoons fresh chopped cilantro, divided
2 dashes Tabasco sauce
½ teaspoon cocoa
½ teaspoon cumin
Pinch cinnamon
Salt and pepper to taste
1 ripe avocado, pitted and peeled
1 tablespoon sour cream
30 small round tortilla chips
¾ cup Monterey Jack cheese with jalapeños, grated
3 Romaine lettuce leaves, thinly shredded

Mash black beans to a coarse consistency with a fork. Combine mashed black beans with garlic, tomatoes, lime zest, 2 tablespoons lime juice, 1 tablespoon cilantro, Tabasco, cocoa, cumin, cinnamon, salt and pepper; mix thoroughly. Place avocado in a separate bowl and mash with 1 tablespoon lime juice and sour cream. Add salt to taste. To serve the tostada bites at room temperature, top each tortilla chip with 1 tablespoon bean mix, ¼ teaspoon avocado mix, grated cheese, shredded lettuce and a sprinkle of chopped cilantro. To serve hot, top each chop with bean mix and cheese. Arrange on a baking sheet and place into a preheated 350° oven for about 5 minutes. Remove to a serving tray and top with avocado mix, lettuce and cilantro.

Eureka Springs Chocolate Lovers Festival

Sausage Pinwheels

1 pound William's hot sausage
1 (8-ounce) package cream cheese, cubed
1 package refrigerated crescent rolls

Crumble and brown sausage over medium heat until very brown and crumbly; drain very well. Stir in cream cheese, until melted. Unwrap crescent rolls—do not separate. Roll into one 15x10-inch rectangle. Spread with sausage mixture. Roll tightly from long side. Slice into 12 rounds. Bake at 375° for 12 to 16 minutes or until brown.

Parker Homestead Festival

Parker Homestead Festival
Second & Third Weekend in October

The Parker Homestead
Harrisburg
870.578.2699
www.parkerhomestead.com

Six miles south of Harrisburg, Arkansas you can find the Parker Pioneer Homestead. This is a recreated 19th century town, complete with buildings and artifacts from times past. Owned and operated by four generations of Parkers, an interest and desire to preserve local history is the driving force behind this living museum. There are many things to see and do at the Homestead, and every October the Parker Homestead Festival celebrates the end of Sorghum harvest season. People from around the state are encouraged to come for a day of history, food and fun. For more information about renting the grounds, having Homestead cater and choreograph your special event, please call or visit our website.

Veggie Snacks

2 (8-ounce) packages refrigerated crescent rolls
2 (8-ounce) packages cream cheese
1 (1-ounce) package dry ranch dressing mix
¼ cup mayonnaise
1 medium red bell pepper, seeded and chopped
½ cup broccoli flowerets
¾ cup shredded Cheddar cheese

Preheat oven to 350°. Roll out crescent rolls and press flat into a 9x13-inch pan. Bake 6 to 8 minutes. Cool completely. Combine cream cheese, dry ranch mix and mayonnaise until smooth. Spread mixture on baked crust. Add chopped vegetables and top with shredded cheese. Cover and chill overnight. Cut into squares and enjoy.

Big Top Caramel Corn

15 cups popped popcorn
1 cup brown sugar, firmly packed
½ cup butter
¼ cup light corn syrup
½ teaspoon salt
½ teaspoon baking soda

Preheat oven to 200°. Place popcorn in a large roasting pan. Heat brown sugar, butter, corn syrup and salt in large saucepan over medium heat, stirring occasionally, until bubbly. Continue cooking for about 5 minutes stirring occasionally. Remove from heat. Stir in baking soda. Pour sugar mixture over popcorn and toss until evenly coated. Bake 1 hour, stirring every 15 minutes. Spread on aluminum foil and allow to cool completely. Store in airtight container.

Celebration Punch

2 cups sugar
2 large cans pineapple juice
3 cans frozen lemonade
1 (3½-ounce) bottle almond extract
½ (3½-ounce) bottle vanilla extract
2 (2-liter) bottles ginger ale

Bring 2 cups water to a boil; stir in sugar. Heat until sugar dissolves; cool. In a large pitcher, add pineapple juice, lemonade, ¾ cup water and extracts. Add sugar water and stir. Chill. Pour over ice in a punch bowl and add ginger ale just before serving.

Summer Sangria

⅔ cup lemon juice
⅓ cup orange juice
¼ cup sugar
1 bottle dry red wine
    (may substitute with nonalcoholic red wine)
Lemon and orange slices

Strain juices into large pitcher. Stir sugar into juices until dissolved. Stir wine into juice mixture and garnish with fruit slices. If desired, add ice.

Almond Crush Punch

2 cups sugar
2 (3-ounce) boxes peach Jell-O
1 ounce (2 tablespoons) almond extract
1 (46-ounce) can pineapple juice

Bring 2 cups water to a full rolling boil; remove from heat. Immediately stir in sugar and Jell-O until well dissolved. Add almond extract, pineapple juice and 10 cups cold water. Mix well. Freeze overnight. Allow to thaw 4 hours before serving. The ideal consistency is frozen, but pourable. Makes 5 quarts or 32 servings.

VW Festival, Swap Meet & Tourcade

Soups, Salads & Breads

Oven Stew

1 (3-pound) chuck roast
5 potatoes or more, peeled and chopped
5 carrots or more, scraped and chopped
5 stalks celery, scraped and chopped
1 tablespoon tapioca
1½ cups sliced onions
2 teaspoons sugar
1 can tomatoes
1 can peas
1 can water
4 beef bouillon cubes
1½ teaspoons Worcestershire sauce

Place all ingredients into a covered roasting dish. Bake at 250° for 5 hours. Do not remove lid while cooking.

Gloria Kruse
Diamond City Festival

Diamond City Festival
Mid-September

Diamond City Community Center
870.422.2668
www.diamondcitychamber.com

The Diamond City Festival has been celebrated for over six years. It is a small street festival featuring hometown entertainment, quilting, chainsaw art and a featured musical artist, usually on Saturday night. A Parade is held on Saturday at 10 a.m. Vendors can rent spaces for as little as $25 and churches and not-for-profits will have fees waived. Past themes have included United We Stand, The Good Old Days, Shine On, and The Renaissance. Diamond City (population 782) is the second largest city in Boone County and is located at the end of Route 7 North, a peninsula jutting out into Bull Shoals Lake. The city features a full-service marina, an 18-hole golf course and lodging in a rustic setting. Camping is available in the Corp of Engineers Park. Come visit The Little City on the Lake.

Turkey Chili

1 pound coarsely ground turkey
1 medium onion, chopped
2 tablespoons olive oil
1 package chili mix
1 (16-ounce) can Rotel
1 (16-ounce) can tomato juice
1 (16-ounce) can chili beans (or kidney beans)

Brown turkey and onions in olive oil. Drain fat and add remaining ingredients. Simmer 15 minutes and enjoy.

The Great Passion Play

Beef or Deer Stew

1 pound stew meat (beef or venison)
4 potatoes, peeled and cut
1 onion, chopped
1 can green beans, with juice
    and any other veggies you would like
1 can tomato soup
1 can whole tomatoes, crushed
Salt and pepper to taste

Layer in order in crockpot. Cook 12 hours on low. Do not stir while cooking.

Jaclyn Curtis
Diamond City Festival

Long Horn Stew

2 pounds hamburger meat, brown and drain
1 can diced tomatoes
1 can Rotel tomatoes
1 can Veg-All
1 can whole-kernel corn
2 cans ranch-style beans
3 cans minestrone soup
1 can water
2 tablespoons Cavender's Greek seasoning

Combine all ingredients in a 6-quart crockpot. Simmer 30 minutes or more. Serve with cornbread, garlic toast or crackers. ENJOY!

Rodeo of the Ozarks

Rodeo of the Ozarks

Downtown Springdale
479.756.0464
www.rodeooftheozarks.com

The Annual Rodeo of the Ozarks in Springdale offers family-friendly entertainment unmatched in the region. The 67th anniversary was celebrated in 2011, and Rodeo of the Ozarks has been honored as one of the top five large outdoor rodeos in the country by the Professional Rodeo Cowboys Association for several consecutive years. The fourth of July festivities are highlighted every year as the world's top cowboys and cowgirls compete in seven PRCA/WPRA sanctioned events: steer wrestling, saddle bronco riding, bareback riding, tie-down roping, team roping, barrel racing and bull riding. Come and enjoy several community events leading up to the Rodeo of the Ozarks including parades downtown, a boot-scootin' street dance, and an amazing fireworks display. For a complete schedule, including some of our other yearly events, please go to our website at www.rodeooftheozarks.org. Come celebrate our nation's heritage with us. There's something for your entire family!

Fruit Soup

4 cups watermelon
1 quart strawberries, cored
1 peach, peeled and pitted
½ cup sugar
1 cup Moscato d'Asti (sparkling white wine)
2 teaspoons salt

Place everything in a blender. Blend until smooth. If using ripe, in-season fruit, this soup should not need adjusting. If, however, one of the fruits is not ripe enough, you may need to add more sugar. The salt in this recipe will bring out the sugar of the fruit, so when adjusting, don't forget to use salt. Alternating salt and sugar will ensure that too much sugar is not added.

Winthrop Rockefeller Institute Saturday Chef's Series

Strawberry Soup

1½ (10-ounce) packages frozen sliced strawberries,
thawed (with juice)
1 (16-ounce) carton sour cream
½ ounce (1 tablespoon) grenadine syrup
3 ounces (⅔ cup) sifted powdered sugar
1 ounce (2 tablespoons) vanilla extract
1 ounce (2 tablespoons) half and half
1 ounce (2 tablespoons) heavy whipping cream

In a mixer, mix strawberries and sour cream together. Beat slowly until well mixed. Add grenadine, vanilla and sugar; stir continuously until mixture becomes smooth. Add half and half and cream last and stir until just blended. Chill and serve. Shake/stir well before serving. Garnish with fresh sliced strawberries. Serves six.

VW Festival, Swap Meet & Tourcade

Chicken Tortilla Soup

2 tablespoons olive oil
1 large onion, chopped
2 tablespoons minced garlic
3 cups chicken broth
1 (14-ounce) can petit-diced tomatoes, undrained
1 (10-ounce) can Rotel tomatoes
1 teaspoon ground cumin
½ teaspoon black pepper
½ teaspoon oregano leaves
1 teaspoon chili powder
⅛ teaspoon paprika
2 cans chili beans, undrained
2 cups chopped, cooked, skinless chicken breasts and/or thighs
1 can summer crisp corn
¼ cup chopped cilantro
Optional garnishes and extra seasonings: tortilla chips, sliced avocados,
   sour cream, shredded Cheddar cheese, Tony Chachere's or Slap Ya
   Mama Cajun spice

Heat olive oil in a Dutch oven over medium heat. Add onion and garlic. Cook until tender, about 6 minutes. Increase heat to high and add broth, tomatoes, Rotel and spices. Reduce heat, cover and simmer about 30 minutes. Add beans and chicken. Add additional chicken broth or water, if necessary. Cook until thoroughly heated. Add corn and cook an additional 5 minutes. Ladle into soup bowl and top with cilantro and your favorite garnishes and extra seasonings.

Cabins in the Ozarks

Bobby's Legendary Beer-Cheese Soup

We always have garlic French bread with this. Perfect for dunking.

2 tablespoons butter
1 small onion, chopped
1 stalk celery, chopped
2 tablespoons flour
¼ teaspoon pepper
¼ teaspoon dry mustard
1 (12-ounce) beer (may substitute with non-alcoholic beer)
1 cup milk
2 cups shredded sharp Cheddar cheese

Melt butter in large saucepan over medium heat. Cook onion and celery until tender. Stir in flour, pepper and mustard. Stir in beer and milk. Heat to boiling over medium heat, stirring constantly, cooking for about 1 minute. Reduce to low heat. Stir in cheese, stirring constantly, until cheese is melted.

Broccoli-Cheese Soup

1 (10-ounce) package frozen broccoli, chopped
1 (15-ounce) can chicken broth
2 teaspoons (or 2 cubes) chicken bouillon
½ cup chopped onion
½ cup chopped celery
Pepper
½ cup milk
2 tablespoons butter or margarine
3 tablespoons cornstarch (with enough milk to dissolve)
2½ to 3 cups shredded Cheddar cheese (or Velveeta)

Boil first 5 ingredients until broccoli is barely tender. Purée in blender about 3 seconds. Add pepper to taste. Return to heat. Add milk, butter, and cornstarch mixture. Blend and stir until hot. Add cheese. Cook until thickened, stirring constantly. Do not boil.

Tomato-Okra Soup

This is perfect served with a grilled cheese sandwich on a cold winter day.

2 cans tomatoes
1 quart fresh or frozen cut-up okra
1 large onion, sliced round
Margarine to taste
½ teaspoon minced garlic
½ teaspoon black pepper
½ teaspoon salt

Put all ingredients into large pan and cover. Bring to a boil; reduce heat to medium. Cook, stirring often, until onions and okra are tender.

Kim's Bean Soup

1 pound Great Northern beans
¼ pound lima beans
1 ham hock
1 beef knuckle bone
1 medium white onion
2 stalks celery, whole
4 cloves garlic, minced
2 teaspoons salt

½ teaspoon pepper
2 (16-ounce) cans stewed tomatoes
¼ cup chopped onions
¼ cup chopped celery
Fresh cilantro, optional
Tabasco, optional
Cooked, shredded chicken, optional
Green onions to garnish

Wash both beans. Cover with water and soak overnight. Drain and cover with fresh water. Bring beans to a boil. Remove from heat and let stand 30 minutes. In another large pot, place ham hock, whole medium onion, whole celery stalks, garlic, salt and pepper. Boil 1 hour; remove celery stalks. Add beans. If necessary, add water to cover beans. Boil slowly several hours until beans are done. Add remaining ingredients; heat. Add salt to taste. Garnish with green onions when serving.

The Elms Plantation

Potato Soup

1 small onion, chopped
3 large white potatoes, diced
¼ cup margarine
1½ teaspoons salt
1 teaspoon pepper
1 cup chicken broth
1 can cream of mushroom soup
1 large can Carnation (evaporated) milk
Water

Melt butter in Dutch oven and sauté chopped onion until limp. Add diced potatoes and enough water to cover. Cook until tender (10 to 15 minutes - watch!). Add salt, pepper, chicken broth and mushroom soup. Stir until mixed well; add milk and bring to a low boil, stirring to prevent sticking. Serve hot. Yum!

Ruth Tate
BPW Barn Sale

Big Dam Bridge

As of 2011, the Big Dam Bridge is the longest pedestrian bridge in United States. The bridge runs north and south between Murray Park and Cook's Landing Park.

Cauliflower Soup

½ head cauliflower, cooked
4 tablespoons butter
2 tablespoons chopped onion
½ teaspoon salt
2 cups half & half
1 large egg yolk
2 tablespoons shredded sharp Cheddar cheese
½ pound bulk sausage, cooked and drained

Pureé cauliflower in a food processor and set aside. Melt butter in Dutch oven. Add onions and cook until tender. Add salt and half & half. Heat thoroughly, but do not boil. Beat egg yolk and add to cream mixture, whipping lightly. Stir in cheese and cauliflower. Mix until well blended. Top each serving with sausage.

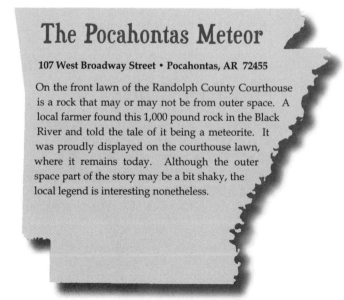

The Pocahontas Meteor

107 West Broadway Street • Pocahontas, AR 72455

On the front lawn of the Randolph County Courthouse is a rock that may or may not be from outer space. A local farmer found this 1,000 pound rock in the Black River and told the tale of it being a meteorite. It was proudly displayed on the courthouse lawn, where it remains today. Although the outer space part of the story may be a bit shaky, the local legend is interesting nonetheless.

Cherry Coke Salad

2 (20-ounce) cans pitted dark cherries
1 (3-ounce) package cherry Jell-O
1 (20-ounce) can crushed pineapple
1 cup Coca-Cola
½ cup chopped pecans

Heat cherries and their juice to boiling. Remove from heat and add Jell-O; stir. Add pineapple, juice and all. Pour in coke and nuts. Pour into an oiled 6-cup mold. Let cool, then refrigerate at least 2 hours or until set. Serve cold.

Randolph County Tourism Association

Wine Country Grape Salad

2 pounds red seedless grapes,
  washed well and dried
1 (8-ounce) package cream cheese, softened
½ cup sugar
1 cup sour cream
½ cup brown sugar
1 cup chopped nuts

Spread grapes evenly in a 9x13-inch pan. Mix cream cheese, sugar and sour cream. Blend until smooth and spread over grapes. Sprinkle with brown sugar and nuts. Refrigerate until serving.

Christ of the Ozarks

Overlooking the beautiful Ozark Mountains is the impressive Christ of the Ozarks. At an altitude of 1500 feet, the seven story, completely handcrafted statue is free to view throughout the year.

Ozark Slaw

1 head cabbage, chopped
½ head purple cabbage, chopped
1 cup grated carrots
1 cup chopped bell pepper (red or yellow makes good color)
1 cup chopped green onions
¼ cup almond slivers
¾ cup sugar
½ cup vegetable oil
2 packages Ramen noodles (chicken flavor)
⅓ cup seasoned rice vinegar
½ tablespoon salt

In large bowl, place all vegetables and almonds. In small pot, put sugar, oil, season packs from Ramen noodles, rice vinegar and salt, warm till sugar dissolves. Set aside to cool. Add Ramen noodles (break apart) to vegetables; stir in oil mixture till all is coated. Let sit 10 minutes and serve.

The Great Passion Play

Jell-O Coleslaw

1 large package lemon Jell-O
½ cup sugar (or sugar substitute like Truvia or Splenda can be substituted)
2 cups boiling water
2 cups mayonnaise
1 (24-ounce) carton cottage cheese
2 tablespoons lemon juice
1 package coleslaw mix

Mix dry Jell-O and sugar. Add boiling water. Allow to cool. Whisk in mayonnaise until smooth. Add cottage cheese, lemon juice and slaw mix. Mix well and put into a 9x13-inch pan and chill.

Mt. Magazine International Butterfly Festival

Vermicelli Salad

1 (16-ounce) package vermicelli
2 to 3 tablespoons light mayonnaise
Morton's Seasoning Nature Blend
1 small package diced ham
½ cup chopped green onion
1 small can chopped black olives, drained
½ small jar capers, drained
1 small carton grape tomatoes, halved
Parmesan cheese

Cook vermicelli according to package directions. Rinse in cold water, drain and set aside. Mix mayonnaise and Morton seasoning to taste. Add ham, onions, olives, tomatoes and capers. Fold in pasta. Sprinkle cheese on top and toss. Serves 8 to 12.

Tour da' Delta

Avocado Shrimp Salad

Dressing:

1 teaspoon prepared mustard
½ teaspoon salt
½ teaspoon pepper
½ teaspoon minced garlic
3 tablespoons wine vinegar
1 small onion, minced
½ cup olive oil
1 tablespoon lemon juice

Salad:

3 ripe avocados
1 can hearts of palm (can use artichoke hearts)
½ pound cooked shrimp
Lettuce, optional

Beat dressing ingredients until mixed well; set aside. Cut each avocado in half, remove seeds, and scoop avocado meat into a bowl. (Reserve avocado shell if you would like to use it as a "bowl" for the finished salad.) Chop hearts of palm and add to bowl. Cut shrimp into thirds; add to bowl. Pour dressing over salad and mix well. Refrigerate until well chilled. Serve over lettuce or spoon into reserved avocado halves.

Carole Fogle, Owner
Morwood House, Jasper
Cabins in the Ozarks

Table Mesa Snap Rocket Spring Pea Salad

4 cups sugar snap peas
2 cups extra virgin olive oil, divided
½ cup fresh lemon juice, divided
Sea salt and fresh ground pepper
3 cups rocket mix (wild arugula)
3 ounces (¾ cup) diced Italian red onion

Lemon zest to taste
1 large English cucumber,
    score with fork and cut in thin round slices
2 cups Parmigiana Reggiano cheese
2 tablespoons honey
½ cup favorite chardonnay

Sauté sugar snap peas with 1.5 ounces (3 tablespoons) olive oil, approximately 2 tablespoons fresh lemon juice, pinch sea salt and fresh ground pepper. Combine greens, snap peas, red onions, lemon zest, cucumbers and cheese; toss. Whisk honey, remaining lemon juice and chardonnay; toss with greens. Plate, drizzle with remaining extra virgin olive oil and grind fresh black pepper over top.

Carl Garrett, Owner, Table Mesa Bistro, Downtown Bentonville
Bentonville Conventions and Visitors Bureau

My Favorite Garden Potato Salad

This is a great side dish or salad to go with chicken, fish or hot dogs. It's perfect for picnics and tailgate parties.

6 medium red potatoes
½ bunch green onions
1 large tomato
1 medium cucumber
½ cup mayonnaise
Salt and pepper to taste

Wash potatoes and leave skins on, cut potatoes into ½ to 1-inch squares, boil in large pot until done. After potatoes are cooked, drain water and let stand until cooled. Chop green onions, tomato, and cucumber. Add to cooled potatoes and mix. Stir in mayonnaise (add more if you like creamier texture), salt and pepper to taste.

Greers Ferry Lake/Little Red River Shoreline Cleanup

Spinach Salad

Salad:

2 packages cut leaf spinach
4 boiled eggs, chopped
1 package green onions, chopped
1 package mushrooms, sliced
4 to 5 slices bacon, cooked and crumbled

Toss together and set aside.

Dressing:

1 cup vegetable oil
¾ cup sugar
⅓ cup ketchup
¼ cup vinegar
2 tablespoons Worcestershire sauce
1 tablespoon sorghum
Salt and pepper to taste

Combine ingredients in saucepan on top of stove. Cook until bubbly. Cool slightly then spoon into mason jar. Pour over salad as needed, shaking occasionally to mix.

Parker Homestead Festival

Brussels Sprout Salad

1½ teaspoons extra-virgin olive oil, divided
1 garlic clove, minced
⅓ cup breadcrumbs
¾ pound Brussels sprouts, trimmed and halved
¼ teaspoon salt
Pepper
⅛ teaspoon finely chopped walnuts, toasted
½ ounce (1 tablespoon) shaved Asiago cheese

Heat 1 teaspoon oil in a large nonstick skillet over medium heat. Add garlic; cook 1 minute or until golden, stirring constantly. Add breadcrumbs and cook another minute, stirring constantly. Put mixture in bowl and set aside. Take leaves from Brussels sprouts and quarter cores. Heat remaining ½ teaspoon oil over medium heat; add Brussels sprouts and toss quickly. Add to breadcrumb mixture along with salt and pepper; toss well. Top with walnuts and cheese.

Fresh Broccoli Cauliflower Salad

6 cups fresh broccoli, cut in pieces
6 cups fresh cauliflower, cut in pieces
2 red onions, thinly sliced
1 tablespoon chopped garlic
2 cups shredded Cheddar cheese
1 (15-ounce) box raisins
1 cup cooked and crumbled bacon
1 cup red wine vinegar
1 cup mayonnaise
½ cup sugar

Wash and cut vegetables; toss together in a large bowl with the garlic, cheese, raisins and bacon. Whisk vinegar, mayonnaise and sugar; toss with vegetables. Marinate in refrigerator 4 hours before serving. Serves 12.

VW Festival, Swap Meet & Tourcade

Tomato and Yellow Squash Salad

2 heirloom tomatoes
Salt and pepper
2 yellow squash
2 tablespoons butter
2 tablespoons chopped parsley
6 bocconcini-size mozzarella balls, quartered
2 tablespoons Smoked Tomato Vinaigrette (see recipe next page)

Slice tomato and season with salt and pepper. Slice squash into medallions. Sauté squash in butter quickly to just soften. Toss with parsley. Layer squash, mozzarella and tomato. Drizzle with vinaigrette.

Winthrop Rockefeller Institute Saturday Chef's Series

Smoked Tomato Vinaigrette

1 cup wood chips
4 heirloom tomatoes
2 to 3 tablespoons cider vinegar
2 tablespoons sugar
1 tablespoon black pepper
2 tablespoons olive oil

Soak wood chips for 1 hour. Drain chips and put into metal roasting pan with cooling rack. Place pan on high heat until wood begins to smoke. Place tomatoes on rack and cover with a cookie tray. Smoke 10 minutes. Put tomatoes, vinegar, sugar, and black pepper into a blender. Pureé until smooth. Slowly add olive oil.

Winthrop Rockefeller Institute Saturday Chef's Series

Saturday Chef's Series
Year Round

Winthrop Rockefeller Institute
Petit Jean Mountain
501.727.5435
www.livethelegacy.org

Winthrop Rockefeller Institute of the University of Arkansas System (commonly called the Rockefeller Institute) is an educational institute and conference center. The legacy of the late Governer Winthrop Rockefeller is kept alive within the Institute by providing educational programs focusing on agriculture, the environment, arts and humanities, economic development, and public affairs. The Saturday Chef's Series offers every "cheficinado" an opportunity to test out and develop new skills and techniques by attending a wholesome, hands-on cooking class at Winthrop Rockefeller Institute. Different local chefs from across the state will teach the class each month. Offering classes on a variety of topics, there is sure to be something tempting for everyone's palate. Space is limited in each class and participation requires advance registration.

Dondie's White River Princess Hushpuppies

2 cups self-rising cornmeal
2 cups self-rising flour
½ teaspoon salt
3 tablespoons sugar
3 large eggs, slightly beaten
½ cup milk
1 large onion, chopped
2 jalapeño peppers, seeded and chopped

Combine first 4 ingredients in large bowl. In a separate bowl, combine eggs and milk. Add to dry ingredients; stir until moistened. Add onions and peppers; mix. Drop by tablespoon into hot oil; cook 3 minutes or until golden brown.

Dondie's White River Princess Restaurant

Lake Chicot

Located in the southeastern Arkanas, Lake Chicot is truly a natural wonder. At 20 miles long, it is the country's largest oxbow lake and Arkansas' largest natural lake. Located in Lake Village, it is a perfect for fishing, boating, and bird watching. Don't miss the self-guided tour — a 30-mile drive that includes a Native American mound and Whiskey Chute where river pirates once roamed.

Purplehull Pea Cornbread

1 pound bulk pork sausage
1 onion, chopped
1 cup white cornmeal
½ cup flour
1 teaspoon salt
½ teaspoon baking soda
2 eggs, slightly beaten
1 cup buttermilk
½ cup vegetable oil
1 (4-ounce) can chopped green chilies, drained
¾ cup cream-style corn
2 cups grated Cheddar cheese
2 cups purplehull peas, cooked

Preheat oven to 350°. Grease a 9x13-inch pan. Cook sausage and onion in large skillet until sausage is browned. Drain and set aside. Combine cornmeal, flour, salt, and baking soda in large bowl. In another bowl, beat eggs, buttermilk, and oil together. Combine with dry ingredients using a few quick strokes (batter does not need to be blended until smooth.) Add sausage with onion, chilies, corn, cheese and purplehull peas. Pour into prepared pan and bake 50 to 55 minutes, or until knife inserted in center comes out clean. Cool and cut into pieces. Serves 8 to 12.

Purplehull Pea Festival
& World Championship Rotary Tiller Race

Zucchini Bread

1 cup oil
2 cups sugar
3 eggs
3 teaspoons vanilla
2 cups shredded raw zucchini
3 cups flour

1 teaspoon baking soda
1 teaspoon salt
3 teaspoons cinnamon
¼ teaspoon baking powder
½ cup chopped nuts

Combine oil, sugar and eggs in a large mixing bowl. Beat well. Blend in vanilla and zucchini. In a separate bowl, stir dry ingredients together. Add to oil mixture and blend well. Add nuts. Pour batter into 2 loaf pans, well greased and lightly floured. Bake at 350° for about an hour. Let stand in pan 10 minutes and then turn out to cool.

Greers Ferry Lake/Little Red River Shoreline Cleanup

Greers Ferry Lake/ Little Red River Shoreline Cleanup
Saturday after Labor Day

Narrows Park in Higden
888.490.4357
www.greersferrylake.org

In 1959, construction began on the Greers Ferry Dam, bringing new jobs, new residents and tourists. Over the next ten years, the new Greers Ferry Lake became a popular recreational spot, and by the millions people came to play, camp, and leave a ton of litter. The Corps of Engineers lacked funds to support a cleanup effort, so a local resident who was with the Corps of Engineers rallied to get the public involved. One Saturday morning in 1970, a team of volunteers, led by Carl Garner, went to work, cleaning the 40,000 acre lake, 200 miles of shoreline, 25 miles of river and 40 miles of roadsides.

In 1984, the Keep Arkansas Beautiful organization adopted Garner's program as the national model for its Public Lands Stewardship program. In 1986, the Federal Lands Cleanup Act was passed, requiring all federal agencies managing federal lands to organize and conduct annual volunteer cleanups every Saturday following Labor Day. Year after year, the Greers Ferry Lake/Little Red River Cleanup continues to be a well-attended event that helps Keep Arkansas Beautiful.

For more information visit us at www.greersferrylake.org or email welcome@greersferrylake.org.

Wild Rice Bread

1 cup warm water
¼ cup molasses
2 tablespoons oil
2 tablespoons brown sugar
1 teaspoon salt
½ cup cooked wild rice
3 cups all-purpose flour
1 teaspoon dry yeast

Put all ingredients in a bread machine in the order listed. Put on dough setting. When done, remove dough and shape in a 9½ x5½-inch greased bread pan. Let rise for 1 to 1½ hours Bake at 350° for 45 minutes.

Bella Vista Arts & Crafts Festival

Garlic Cheese Dinner Biscuits

2½ cups self-rising flour
½ cup shortening
¾ cup milk
1 cup shredded sharp Cheddar cheese

Preheat oven to 450°. Put flour in a large bowl and put shortening on top in very small pieces. Gradually stir in milk and cheese, mixing enough to just moisten flour and form dough. Drop by rounded spoonfuls onto baking sheet. Bake 8 to 9 minutes or until golden brown.

Garlic Butter:
¼ cup butter, softened
½ teaspoon garlic powder

Combine butter and garlic powder until well blended. Brush tops of biscuits.

Dutch Oven Biscuits

2 cups flour
½ teaspoon salt
3 teaspoons baking powder
4 tablespoons solid shortening
1 cup milk (diluted canned milk is okay)

Blend flour, salt and baking powder. Mash in shortening with a fork until crumbly. Add milk and stir until the dough sags down into trough left by spoon as it moves around the bowl. Turn dough out on a floured surface, knead for 30 seconds, pat out gently until it is ½-inch thick. Cut with a round cutter or pinch off pieces of dough and form by hand. Put biscuits into a greased Dutch oven, cover, and bury in bright coals for 5 or 10 minutes or until golden brown.

Chocolate Gravy

1 cup sugar
3 heaping tablespoons flour
2 tablespoons Hershey's cocoa
2½ cups water

In a small saucepan, mix dry ingredients well. Add water. Bring to a boil over medium-high heat. Boil until thick. Serve over biscuits or toast.

Diamond City Festival

Super Quick Dinner Rolls

1 cup self-rising flour
½ cup milk
2 tablespoons mayonnaise

Preheat oven to 350°. If you are not using a nonstick muffin pan, grease 5 cups of a regular muffin pan. In a medium bowl, stir together all ingredients. Spoon into the 5 prepared muffin cups. Bake 15 minutes in preheated oven, or until nicely puffed and browned.

Ham and Cheese Corn Muffins

1 ⅔ cups all-purpose flour
1 cup yellow cornmeal
1 tablespoon sugar
1¼ teaspoons baking soda
½ teaspoon salt
⅛ teaspoon ground red pepper
1¼ cups buttermilk
2 eggs, beaten
3 tablespoons canola oil
¾ cup shredded sharp Cheddar cheese
½ cup chopped green onion
½ cup frozen whole-kernel corn
⅓ cup chopped ham

Preheat oven to 350°. Combine flour, cornmeal, sugar, baking soda, salt and red pepper in large bowl. In a separate bowl, combine buttermilk, eggs and oil. Add to flour mixture, stirring until moist. Fold in cheese, green onions, corn and diced ham. Grease 12 muffin cups and spoon batter into each. Bake 22 minutes. Cool completely.

The World's Largest Tuned Musical Wind Chime

Just south of Eureka Springs on Highway 23 is the World's Largest Tuned Musical Wind Chimes. Certified by Guinness Book of World's Records in 2006, the musical wonder was crafted by Ranaga Farbiarz and is located in the parking lot of The Celestial Windz Harmonic Bazaar. Stop by, give a dollar, and give a big ring on the largest chime you've ever seen.

Blueberry Muffins

3½ cups flour
2 cups sugar
1½ teaspoons salt
1 teaspoon baking soda
4 eggs, slightly beaten

1 cup Wesson oil
1 teaspoon vanilla
¼ teaspoon almond extract
2 cups frozen blueberries
1 cup chopped almonds

Blend dry ingredients together well in a mixing bowl. Add eggs, oil, vanilla and almond extract; mix together well. Add blueberries and almonds at the end; stir until just mixed. Ladle batter into a greased muffin tin and bake at 325° for 20 to 22 minutes. Makes 30 to 36.

VW Festival, Swap Meet & Tourcade

VW Festival Swap Meet & Tourcade
Fourth Weekend in August

**Inn of the Ozarks
Eureka Springs
479.253.9768
www.nwavwa.com**

In 1993 the North West Volkswagen Association formed and the Volkswagen Festival and Tourcade was born. Held every year on the fourth weekend in August, VW enthusiasts from all parts of the country descend on the picturesque downtown area of Eureka Springs.

The festivities are kicked off with a BBQ cookout for all pre-registered participants. Saturday is filled with activity for the car show and swap meet. VW's are proudly displayed and entries are judged in twenty-six different categories. Residents and visitors alike wait for the VW parade to begin, and as the VW's wind through the rustic streets, the crowd gives encouraging cheers, hoping to hear the welcoming beep-beep of the Volkswagen horn. The festival ends on Sunday with a countryside VW tourcade through some of the most scenic areas of Northern Arkansas one could ever hope to see.

The Volkswagen Festival and Tourcade is a premier Volkswagen extravaganza, worth coming back to year after year.

Light-as-Air Lemon Poppy Seed Muffins

1 whole lemon
1 cup sugar
½ cup vegetable oil
⅔ cup milk
2 eggs
1 tablespoon poppy seeds
1 teaspoon vanilla
2 cups all-purpose flour
1 tablespoon baking powder
1 teaspoon salt
½ cup powdered sugar

Preheat oven to 350°. Grease muffin pan. Wash and dry the lemon, and grate a bit of rind off carefully. Set rind aside. Cut the lemon in half and squeeze out juice from both sides. Set juice aside. Combine sugar and vegetable oil in large bowl. Add milk, eggs, poppy seeds, vanilla and lemon rind. Mix thoroughly. In another bowl, mix flour, baking powder and salt. Add the egg mixture and stir very well. Spoon batter into muffin tins, filling each cup about ⅔ full. Bake 20 minutes or until a toothpick inserted in the center comes out clean. In a small mixing bowl, mix lemon juice and powdered sugar. Pour lemon glaze evenly over muffins and allow to cool in pan.

Banana Nut Bread

¾ cup butter or margarine
1½ cups sugar
2 eggs
1 cup pecans
2 cups self-rising flour
4 well-ripened bananas, mashed

Combine all ingredients one at a time. Mix well. Pour into greased and floured loaf pans or Bundt pan. Bake at 350° for 45 to 60 minutes or until toothpick inserted in center comes out clean (Bundt pan will need to cook longer).

Toad Suck Daze
First Weekend in May

Conway
501.327.7788
www.toadsuck.org

Long ago, steamboats traveled the Arkansas River when the water was the right depth. When it wasn't, the captains and their crews tied up to wait where the Toad Suck Ferry Lock and Dam now span the river. While they waited, they refreshed themselves at the tavern. The dismayed folks living nearby were heard to say: 'They suck on the bottle 'til they swell up like toads.' Hence Toad Suck. The tavern is long gone, but the legend still lives on at Toad Suck Daze. The first weekend in May over 150,000 people come to downtown Conway to attend Toad Suck Daze. For over 30 years, this festival's atmosphere of family, food and fun has made Toad Suck Daze a favorite with Arkansans as well as visitors from around the World. Toad Suck Daze activities include: Toad Market Arts & Crafts, Carnival, 5K/10K Race, Toadal Kids Zone, Live Entertainment and of course the World Famous Championship Toad Races. Besides being one of the most popular festivals in Arkansas, Toad Suck Daze also has provided over $1 Million in scholarship money since its beginning.

Market Fresh Strawberry Bread

3 cups strawberries, fresh or frozen
3 cups flour
2 cups sugar
1¼ teaspoons cinnamon
1 teaspoon baking soda
1 teaspoon salt
1¼ cups oil
4 eggs, beaten

Preheat oven to 350°. Mash and drain strawberries, reserving ½ cup juice. Mix dry ingredients in a large bowl. Add strawberries, juice, oil and eggs. Mix well. Pour into 2 greased loaf pans. Bake 50 to 60 minutes. Cool completely before serving.

Vegetables & Other Side Dishes

Razorback Veggie Kabobs

Serve these on game day.

2 red bell peppers, cut into ½-inch strips
2 small zucchini, cut into ½-inch slices
1 large white or red onion, halved
 and cut into ½-inch wedges
8 (6-inch) bamboo skewers,
 soaked in water for several minutes

¼ cup olive oil
2 tablespoons lemon juice
2 tablespoons white wine vinegar
1 teaspoon Italian seasoning
½ teaspoon salt

Put peppers, zucchini and onion onto bamboo skewers and place in a shallow dish. Set aside. Combine oil and remaining ingredients and pour over kebobs. Cover and refrigerate overnight, turning once. Grill over medium-hot coals 10 to 15 minutes, turning and brushing occasionally with marinade.

Grilled Veggie Sandwiches

Dressing:

1 garlic clove, minced
4 teaspoons mayonnaise
1 teaspoon mustard
Dash Worcestershire sauce
Salt and pepper, to taste

Mix all ingredients together. Set aside.

Sandwiches:

2 teaspoons oil
4 slices zucchini
2 good-quality mushrooms, sliced
½ green or red bell pepper, sliced
½ avocado, sliced
¼ cup shredded Cheddar cheese
4 slices white or wheat bread, toasted

Heat oil in frying pan over medium heat. Add zucchini, mushrooms and peppers. Sauté 3 to 5 minutes. Reduce heat to low. Add avocado and cheese and cook just 30 seconds. Remove from heat. Spoon ½ on a slice of toast. Top with dressing and another slice of bread. Repeat. Serves 1 to 2.

Brunch Burritos

1 large green bell pepper, chopped
⅔ cup chopped onion
2 tablespoons butter or margarine
8 eggs, slightly beaten

1 cup shredded Cheddar cheese
1½ cups picante sauce
8 (8-inch) flour tortillas
Sour cream (optional)

In 10-inch skillet, cook green pepper and onion in butter. Combine eggs and cheese; add to skillet. Cook over medium heat, stirring frequently, until eggs are set and cheese is melted. Heat picante sauce in small skillet until warm. Dip each tortilla into picante sauce. Spoon about ½ cup egg mixture onto center of each tortilla. Fold 2 sides over egg mixture; fold ends under and place in 9x13-inch baking dish. Top with remaining picante sauce. Bake at 350° until hot, about 10 minutes. Top with sour cream, if desired. Makes 6 to 8 servings.

Arkansas Air Museum

4290 South School Street • Fayetteville
479.521.4947 • www.arkairmuseum.org

The history of manned flight is proudly on display at the Arkansas Air Museum. Holding the title as the state's oldest museum, the all-wood, White Hangar is the home of a one-of-a-kind collection. From world-famous racing planes of the 1920s and 1930s to an early airliner, the historic aircraft in the Arkansas Air Museum are unusual among museum exhibits, because many of them still fly. The special history of Arkansas aviation is proudly told through the photos and  portraits of the Arkansas Aviation Hall of Fame. Want to see how these historic craft are returned to glory? The restoration of these gems of the sky can be seen in the restoration shop. Visit the website for current exhibits, hours and rates, and we look forward to meeting the whole family.

Get-Ready-for-the-Race Breakfast

1 cup plain yogurt
1 cup orange or pineapple juice
½ teaspoon vanilla
1 large banana
1 tablespoon honey (optional)

Place all ingredients in a blender or food processor and blend until smooth.

All Sports Productions, Inc.

All Sports Productions, Inc.

Races occur throughout the year

1629 South River Meadows Drive
Fayetteville
479.521.7766
www.allsportsproductionsinc.com

Arkansas has the ideal climate and terrain for outdoor activities of all kinds, and All Sports Productions, Inc. brings a competitive edge to the Natural State. All Sports Productions, Inc. is a sports event management and consulting company which promotes cycling, running, triathlons, and other outdoor races. The goal of the company is to produce local, regional and nationally recognized events at the highest standards with a festival-like atmosphere. The mission of each event is to engage new participants and spectators in a healthy, multi-sport lifestyle. Below is a small sampling of the races held each year: Iron Pig Festival—duathlon, 5K run, fun run/walk and bike time trial; Joe Martin Stage Race—professional and amateur bicycle races; Tri-Sport Kid Family Triathlon—pool swim, bike and run; Ozark Valley Triathlon—1,000 yard swim, 19 mike bike, 4 mile run; Eureka Springs Multisport Festival The Eurekon; Lewis & Clark Adventure Races; Fayetteville Half Marathon—half marathon, 5K, 1 mile race and fun run. Be sure to visit www.allsportsproductionsinc.com or call 479.521.7766 for details on these events and to discover other races. Get ready to compete!

Squash Relish

10 cups chopped squash, yellow or green
3 tablespoons salt
4 cups chopped onion
4 cups sugar
2½ cups vinegar
2 tablespoons cornstarch
2 teaspoons celery seed
1 teaspoon dry mustard
1 teaspoon nutmeg
1 teaspoon turmeric
½ teaspoon black pepper

Mix squash and salt, and let stand overnight. Drain and rinse well with cold water. Add remaining ingredients. Cook at a rolling boil 3 minutes. Put in hot sterilized jars and seal. Makes 6 to 8 pints.

Emily Jackson
Diamond City Festival

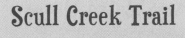

Scull Creek Trail

The 4.4 mile Scull Creek Trail runs north and south through the heart of Fayetteville. This trail is well-lit, paved, and connects with many of Fayetteville's other trails. This picturesque trail is suitable for walkers, runners, and bikers of all types.

Green Beans with New Potatoes

3 pounds fresh green beans
¼ pound bacon
2 to 2½ cups chicken broth
2 to 3 teaspoons seasoned salt
12 small red potatoes, washed well and in the skins
1 onion, sliced
½ stick butter, sliced
Black pepper, to taste

Snap beans (remove ends and break in 2 pieces), wash and set aside. In a large saucepan, lightly brown bacon. Add green beans and stir to coat with bacon grease. Add chicken broth and seasoned salt. Cook over medium-low heat, covered tightly, for approximately 30 minutes (beans should only be half done). Add potatoes and onion; add ¼ cup more broth if needed. Cook, covered tightly, until potatoes are tender, about 25 to 30 minutes (check occasionally and add water or additional chicken broth as needed). Uncover; add butter and black pepper. Continue to cook until beans are completely wilted. Serves 8 to 10.

Grandma's Famous Baked Beans

2 cups dried navy beans, sorted and rinsed
½ cup firmly packed brown sugar
¼ cup molasses
1 teaspoon salt
6 slices bacon, cooked and crumbled
1 medium onion, chopped

Preheat oven to 350°. Add beans to 10 cups water and bring to a boil. Boil, uncovered, for 2 minutes. Stir in remaining ingredients. Cover and cook 4 hours, stirring occasionally. Stir in 3 cups water and cook uncovered for 2 hours, stirring occasionally, until beans are tender.

Creole Green Beans

1 (16-ounce) package frozen cut green beans
5 slices bacon
1 medium onion, chopped
½ cup chopped green bell pepper
2 tablespoons flour
2 tablespoons brown sugar
1 tablespoon Worcestershire sauce
1 teaspoon salt
½ teaspoon pepper
½ teaspoon ground mustard
1 (14½-ounce) can diced tomatoes, undrained

Cook beans according to package directions. In a skillet, cook bacon, onion and green pepper over medium heat until bacon is crisp and vegetables are tender. Remove with slotted spoon; set aside. Stir flour, brown sugar, Worcestershire sauce, salt, pepper and mustard into drippings until blended. Stir in tomatoes. Bring to a boil; cook and stir 2 minutes. Drain beans and add to skillet. Stir in bacon mixture. Makes 6 servings.

Diane Thompson for Irene Casalino
Cas-Kee Cabin, Marble Falls
Cabins in the Ozarks

Bayou Bartholomew

Arkansas is home to many interesting people, places and things. Bayou Bartholmew is definitely one of them. At 350 miles long, it is the longest bayou in the world. Over 100 species of fish have been identifed within Bayou Bartholmew making it a supreme fishing spot in The Natural State.

Queen's Green Beans

3 (14½-ounce) cans whole green beans
4 thin slices bacon, cooked and crumbled
    (reserve 2 tablespoons drippings)
1 large onion, chopped
3 garlic cloves, minced
1 (2-ounce) jar diced pimento, drained
¼ cup red wine vinegar
1 teaspoon sugar
½ teaspoon salt
½ teaspoon pepper
½ teaspoon cumin seeds (optional)

Drain green beans. Set aside. Sauté onion and garlic in bacon drippings. Stir in pimento, vinegar, sugar, salt, pepper and cumin. Add green beans and combine gently. Simmer about 5 minutes. Sprinkle with bacon. Makes 6 to 8 servings.

Whistlestop Festival

Whistlestop Festival
First Weekend in May

Downtown Ashdown
903.280.2944 or 870.898.9080
www.littlerivercounty.org

A perfect stop for any railroad enthusiast, the annual Whistlestop Festival is located in the center of historic downtown Ashdown. Whether you stroll up and down the streets filled with antique shops and craft vendors or run in the 5K, 10K, or half-marathon, you will work up an appetite to eat from any of the several food vendors while enjoying local entertainment. The event also features the Hook 'Em and Kook 'Em Catfish and Hushpuppy Cook-Off with hefty prize money awarded to the winners. It is the season opening of the Farmers Market, located across the street from the historic GN&A Railroad depot and historic caboose, both open for tours. Join us each year as we celebrate with fun and entertainment for both children and adults at the Whistlestop Festival!

Braised Whippoorwill Peas

10 ounces peas
Chicken stock
1 ounce (1 slice) bacon
2 ounces (½ to ¾ cup) onion
2 ounces (¼ cup) Smoked Tomato Vinaigrette (see page 58)
2 bay leaves
2 thyme sprigs

Simmer peas in enough stock to cover by three inches until almost tender (drain and save liquid). Render bacon fat in a large saucepan; add onion and sauté until brown. Add peas, tomatoes, bay leaf, thyme, and enough liquid to moisten, bring to a simmer. Cover pot and braise in a 350° oven until peas absorb the liquid, about 30 minutes. To finish, season with salt and pepper.

Winthrop Rockefeller Institute Saturday Chef's Series

Baked Onions

4 large yellow onions
½ cup butter
Tony Chachere's unsalted
   Creole Seasoning to taste

Preheat oven to 325°. Remove top and bottom from each onion. Cut criss-cross pattern into tops, leaving about ½ inch on the bottom intact. Stuff each onion with 2 tablespoons butter and sprinkle with seasoning. Place in greased casserole and bake, covered, for 1 hour or until onion is translucent.

Onion Rings

4 large mild yellow onions,
    sliced ¼-inch thick and separated into rings
⅔ cup buttermilk
1 cup cornmeal
1 cup flour
Salt and pepper to taste

Soak onions in buttermilk. Combine cornmeal, flour, salt and pepper. Dredge soaked onions in dry mixture. Fry in oil heated to 350° until golden brown.

Carla Mitchell
Historic Oark General Store & Cafe

Historic Oark General Store & Cafe

215 Main Street • Oark
479.292.3351 • www.oarkgeneralstore.com

Historic Oark General Store was established in 1890 and is listed on the Register of Historic Places in Arkansas. Serving the area for over one hundred and twenty years, this is the oldest store in Arkansas in continuous operation. The building has the original floors, walls and ceiling. Shelves are always stocked with goods to support the needs of the community including groceries, cigarettes, hardware, gasoline and automotive supplies, gifts and souvenirs. We also have picnic and camping items, a few over-the-counter medications and personal care needs. We also offer home-cooked breakfast, lunch and dinner daily, featuring our famous ½ lb. hamburgers, steaks, catfish, daily lunch specials and much more. Don't forget to save room for a piece of homemade pie and hand-dipped ice cream. The store is located 22 miles from Clarksville. Take Hwy 103 North to where it turns into Hwy 215. Go another mile to get to the Historic Oark General Store.

Carrots with Cheese

1 large bag frozen sliced carrots
1 small onion, diced
8 ounces Velveeta, cubed
½ cup breadcrumbs
½ stick margarine

Cook carrots according to directions; drain. Mix carrots with mixer. Add onion and cheese. Mix well. Put into greased casserole dish. Sprinkle with breadcrumbs. Tab margarine on top. Cook 15 minutes at 350°. Broil at the end to toast breadcrumbs.

Wildflower Bed & Breakfast on the Square

Black Pepper Caramel Carrots

2½ tablespoons butter
2½ tablespoons packed light brown sugar
¼ teaspoon kosher salt
1 pound baby carrots, halved lengthwise
1 tablespoon freshly ground black pepper

Heat butter, sugar, and salt over medium-high heat; stir well until smooth. Add carrots and toss to coat. Cover and reduce heat to medium-low. Simmer 15 minutes or until carrots are tender and well-glazed. Top with black pepper. Serves 4.

Farmers Market Broiled Tomatoes

3 large fresh tomatoes, cut in half crosswise
Salt and freshly ground pepper
2 tablespoons butter
2 tablespoons chopped fresh parsley
2 tablespoons Italian dressing (bottled or homemade vinaigrette)
3 tablespoons grated Romano cheese

Sprinkle salt and pepper on the cut side of each tomato half. Broil 4 minutes, about 4 inches from heat. Remove from broiler. On each tomato half, place 1 teaspoon butter, 1 teaspoon chopped parsley, 1 teaspoon dressing and 1 generous teaspoon Romano cheese. Return to broiler for 2 minutes. Serve immediately.

Beebe Fall Festival
Third Week in October

Downtown Beebe
501.827.0353
www.beebeark.org

If traveling through the central part of the state during the third week in October, it will be worthwhile to veer a little to the Northeast and visit Beebe. Named after Roswell Beebe, a railroad executive responsible for bringing the rail line to the city, this small town offers big fun each year with the Beebe Fall Festival. The Beebe Chamber of Commerce works diligently throughout the year to put together this fall celebration. Held in downtown

Lee McLane/The Beebe News

Beebe, there are antique cars, live music, games, food and entertainment. A fun-filled day for the entire family, the Beebe Fall Festival is a tradition for residents and a treasure for travelers. Visit www.beebeark.org or call 501.882.8135 for details and directions.

Baked Spinach and Eggs

2½ pounds fresh spinach
½ cup butter, divided
¼ cup grated Parmesan cheese
6 eggs
Salt and pepper

Preheat oven to 375°. Bring ¼ cup water to a rapid boil in a large skillet. Wash spinach well under cold running water; remove any heavy stalks. When water is boiling, add spinach and salt to taste. Cook 7 minutes. Drain well and squeeze dry with paper towel. Set aside. Dry skillet and melt 4 tablespoons butter over medium high heat. Add spinach and sauté several minutes. Grease an oven-safe casserole or baking dish with 1 tablespoon butter. Transfer spinach to baking dish. Sprinkle evenly with Parmesan cheese. Melt remaining butter and pour over spinach. Bake 30 minutes are until cheese has thoroughly melted. Meanwhile, sauté eggs seasoned with salt and pepper to taste. Serve spinach with eggs on a heated serving dish.

Oven-Roasted Vegetables

⅓ cup olive oil
2 to 3 tablespoons fresh rosemary, thyme, basil or herbes de provence
Carrots, cut into 2-inch pieces
Zucchini, cut diagonally into pieces ½ inch thick
Sweet potatoes, cut into pieces ½ inch thick
Bell peppers, cut into 2-inch pieces
Asparagus, trimmed
Onions, cut into quarters
Eggplant, cut diagonally into ½-inch slices
Salt to taste

Combine olive oil and rosemary in a bowl and mix well. Let stand 1 hour or longer. Combine carrots, zucchini, sweet potatoes, bell peppers, asparagus, onions and eggplant or your favorite combination of vegetables in a large bowl. Add olive oil mixture and toss to coat well. Arrange in a single layer in a shallow roasting pan. Sprinkle with salt. Bake at 500° for 8 minutes. Reduce oven temperature to 400°. Bake for 6 to 8 minutes or until the vegetables are tender when pierced with a knife.

Junior League of Pine Bluff
Pine Bluff Convention and Visitors Bureau

White Pizza

2 large home-made or ready-made pizza crusts (or 4 small)
1 pound plum tomatoes, thinly sliced
1 onion, peeled and sliced
1 (3-ounce) package watercress, finely chopped
4 ounces ricotta cheese
1 tablespoon fresh green peppercorns
1 (4-ounce) package mozzarella, small cubes
4 ounces cherry tomatoes, halved
Sprigs of basil for garnish

Preheat oven to 425°. Arrange plum tomato slices over pizza crusts. Gently fry onion 4 to 5 minutes and sprinkle over tomatoes with the watercress. Spoon ricotta on top. Add peppercorns, then mozzarella and cherry tomatoes. Bake 20 to 25 minutes. Garnish with basil and serve.

Spinach Quiche

9 eggs
3 cups milk
½ teaspoon salt
1 teaspoon pepper
9 slices bread, cubed
1 box frozen spinach
2 cups mozzarella cheese

Beat eggs and milk together; add salt and pepper and mix. Grease or Pam a 9x13-inch casserole dish. Layer bread cubes in bottom of dish. Layer spinach over bread. Pour egg mixture over bread and spinach. Layer cheese on top. Cover and refrigerate overnight. Heat oven to 350°. Bake 50 minutes or until done.

Diane Novotny
Jacksonville Parks and Recreation

Cheese & Spinach Pie

3 large eggs, beaten
6 tablespoons flour
10 ounces fresh or frozen spinach
2 cups cottage cheese
1½ cups shredded Cheddar cheese

Preheat oven to 350°. Combine egg and flour in a mixing bowl; beat until smooth. Fold in the spinach then cottage cheese. Stir in shredded cheese. Spoon into a greased 9-inch pie plate or square baking dish. Bake 45 minutes. Serve hot or cold with your favorite fish or meat dish.

Mt. Magazine International Butterfly Festival

Cotham's Fried Green Tomatoes

Green tomatoes
  (if the tomatoes are starting to turn, they will not work)
Cotham's Catfish Seasoning or seasoned cornmeal
Oil

Slice tomatoes about ⅛-inch thick (or to your preference). Soak in ice water for about 5 minutes. Heat at least an inch of oil in skillet or deep fryer to 350°. Take tomatoes out of water, coat with catfish seasoning or cornmeal, and fry about 8 minutes, turning once. Remove to paper towel to drain. Serve with your favorite dressing (the restaurant prefers ranch).

Cotham's Restaurant, Scott and Little Rock

The Old Mill

The Old Mill located outside of North Little Rock is said to be the only remaining structure from the film *Gone with the Wind*. The quiet and picturesque setting will take you back to a simpler time.

Green Tomato Pie

Crust:

2¼ cups biscuit mix (like Bisquick)
½ teaspoon dried thyme
½ cup milk

Combine biscuit mix and thyme. Quickly stir in milk with a fork until just blended. Press dough into a greased 10-inch pie plate.

Filling:

1 small onion, thinly sliced
6 green tomatoes, peeled and sliced
1 teaspoon sugar
Salt and pepper to taste
2 tablespoons chopped basil
2 tablespoons chopped chives
2 cups mayonnaise
1 teaspoon lemon juice
2 cups shredded cheese

Preheat oven to 350°. Into crust arrange onion slices, tomato slices, sugar, salt, pepper and herbs. Mix mayonnaise, lemon juice and cheese together and spread over tomatoes. Bake 30 to 40 minutes, until golden and bubbly. May be served hot or at room temperature.

Mt. Magazine International Butterfly Festival

Broccoli Puff

2 (10-ounce) packages frozen chopped broccoli, cooked and drained
1 cup medium white sauce
1 cup mayonnaise
2 tablespoons minced onion
1½ teaspoons salt
1 teaspoon lemon juice
¼ teaspoon pepper
6 eggs, beaten

Mix all ingredients and turn them into a buttered casserole. Place in a shallow pan of water. Bake at 325° for 1 hour or until knife inserted in center comes out clean. Serves 8.

White Sauce: Melt 1 tablespoon butter, add 1 tablespoon all-purpose flour to make a paste, and add 1 cup milk cooking until thick, stirring constantly.

Hot Springs Arts & Crafts Fair

Isabel Poulin

Hot Springs Arts & Crafts Fair
First Weekend in October

Garland County Fairgrounds
Hot Springs
501.623.9592 or 501.922.9186
www.hotspringsartsandcraftsfair.com

The Hot Springs Arts and Crafts Fair is traditionally held at the Garland County Fairgrounds annually on the first full weekend (a Friday, Saturday and Sunday) in October. Residents of Hot Springs and surrounding areas consider The Arts and Crafts Fair to be the official "kickoff" event heralding the rapidly approaching Christmas season. It is one of the oldest and largest arts and crafts fairs in the state of Arkansas. The history of the Hot Springs Arts & Crafts Fair is almost as rich and colorful as the city of Hot Springs itself. The Fair has grown into an event for the entire family and features great fair food, pony rides and a petting zoo for children.

Sweet Potato Casserole

Topping:
½ cup flour
½ cup melted butter
1 tablespoon sorghum
1 cup brown sugar
1 cup chopped pecans

Combine all topping ingredients and set aside.

Sweet Potato Casserole:
3 cups cooked sweet potatoes
1 stick butter
½ cup heavy cream
1 cup brown sugar
2 eggs
1 tablespoon vanilla
1 tablespoon sorghum

Mash potatoes with butter and cream. Add remaining ingredients, beating well. Pour into casserole dish and cover with topping. Bake 30 minutes at 300°. Topping will be crunchy.

Parker Homestead Festival

Corn Casserole

1 (15¼-ounce) can whole-kernel corn, drained
1 (14¾-ounce) can cream-style corn
1 (8-ounce) package corn muffin mix (Jiffy)
1 cup sour cream
½ cup (1 stick) butter, melted
1 cup shredded Cheddar cheese

Combine all ingredients, except cheese. Pour into a greased casserole. Bake at 350°for 40 to 45 minutes, or until golden brown. Top cheese and return to oven for another 5 minutes or until cheese is melted. Serves 6 to 8.

Cheesy Corn Pie

3 eggs, beaten
⅓ cup cream or half-and-half
1 teaspoon salt
⅛ teaspoon pepper
1 tablespoon grated onion
2 cups cooked whole-kernel corn (or 1 can)
1 cup grated sharp Cheddar cheese
6 strips bacon, partially cooked
1 (9-inch) pie crust

Preheat oven to 400°. Combine eggs, cream, salt and pepper; beat until smooth. Add onion, corn and cheese; pour into unbaked pie crust. Place bacon over top, arranging in a pretty design. Bake 25 to 30 minutes.

The Clinton Presidential Library & Museum

Located on the banks of the Arkansas River in the River Market District of downtown Little Rock is the William J. Clinton Presidential Center and Park. Within the center is 20,000 square feet of library and museum space. In addition to the preserved documents and artifacts on display, waiting to be discovered is an identical replica of the Oval Office and Cabinet room.

Squash Casserole

1 pound yellow squash, sliced
¼ cup chopped onion
1 tablespoon sugar
3 tablespoons butter
1 cup grated cheese, divided
2 eggs, beaten
¼ teaspoon sage
Salt to taste

Mix squash and onions and cook in covered pan until tender (no water and don't overcook). Drain and add sugar, butter, ½ cup cheese, eggs, sage and salt. Put in greased casserole dish. Add rest of cheese on top and bake at 325° for 25 minutes.

Elaine Scudder, Little Rock Farmers' Market
Jane and Elaine's Plants and Produce

River Market Farmers' Market

River Market Pavilions • Downtown Little Rock
501.375.2552 • www.rivermarket.info

Patronized by locals and tourists alike, the Farmers' Market has served as a seasonal institution and local destination favorite since it opened in 1974. Filled with farmers selling farm-fresh produce straight to consumers from the backs of their trucks, patrons can find bargains on Arkansas crops as well as a bountiful array of handmade arts and crafts. Over 200 vendors participate in Little Rock's Farmers' Market each year and this regional market is the largest in the state. Several of the farm families have been selling their produce and products since it began and some travel  as far as 90 miles to participate. The Farmers' Market makes its home in the River Market's two outdoor, open-air pavilions overlooking Riverfront Park and the Arkansas River. The Farmers' Market is open every Tuesday and Saturday from May through October, 7:00 a.m. to 3:00pm. For more information, visit www.rivermarket.info or call the River Market at 501.375.2552.

Cabbage Casserole

1 large head cabbage, shredded
1 teaspoon salt
½ stick margarine
3 cups Basic White Sauce (see recipe that follows)
2 cups grated Cheddar cheese
1½ cups buttered breadcrumbs

Cook cabbage 5 to 8 minutes in boiling water with 1 teaspoon salt. Don't overcook; cabbage should remain crisp. Drain well. Layer ½ cabbage in buttered 2-quart casserole. Add white sauce to cover. Repeat layers with remaining cabbage and white sauce. Top with cheese and buttered breadcrumbs. Bake in preheated 300° oven 15 to 20 minutes. Serves 8 to 10.

Basic White Sauce:
3 tablespoons butter
3 tablespoons all-purpose flour
Salt and pepper to taste
3 cups milk

Melt margarine in saucepan; add flour, salt and pepper to make a paste. Add milk and cook until thick, stirring constantly.

The World's Largest Can of Spinach

When traveling through the western part of the state on Interstate 40, look over the fields and you are likely to spot the World's Largest Can of Popeye Spinach. A great opportunity for a unique photo!

Garden Casserole

4 cups fresh or frozen veggies, cut small
(or 2 16-ounce cans mixed veggies, drained)
Salt and pepper
1 medium onion, chopped small
1 can water chestnuts, chopped or minced

16 ounces Cheddar or Velveeta cheese,
grated or cubed
1 to 1½ cups mayonnaise
1 tube Ritz cracker, crushed
½ stick butter or margarine, melted

Preheat oven to 350°. Steam or boil fresh or frozen veggies (cook only until almost tender); add salt and pepper to taste. (Suggested veggies: peas, green beans, carrots, potatoes, corn, etc.) In a large bowl, combine veggies, onion, water chestnuts, cheese and mayonnaise. Add just enough mayonnaise to bind it together. Place in well-greased or buttered 9x13-inch pan and bake 30 minutes or until bubbly. Remove from oven and top with crushed Ritz crackers. Melt butter and drizzle over crackers. Return to oven until brown.

Pam and Friends
Conway EcoFest

Roasted Zucchini with Ricotta and Mint

Flavored with fennel and cumin seeds, this quick side dish (or vegetarian main course) has a fun Indian flavor. While chef Sheamus Feeley likes to add pequin peppers, any chile flakes work well.

8 medium zucchini (3 pounds), cut into ½-inch dice
Extra-virgin olive oil, plus more for drizzling
Kosher salt and freshly ground black pepper
1 teaspoon crushed red pepper
½ teaspoon cumin seeds
½ teaspoon fennel seeds
2 teaspoons fresh lemon juice
Fresh ricotta, for serving
Mint leaves, for garnish

Preheat oven to 450°. Spread diced zucchini on 2 large rimmed baking sheets. Drizzle with olive oil and season with salt and black pepper to taste. Roast about 18 minutes, until zucchini are browned around edges. Sprinkle zucchini with crushed red pepper, cumin seeds and fennel seeds; roast until fragrant, about 2 minutes longer. Transfer zucchini to a bowl. Toss with lemon juice and season with salt to taste. Dollop ricotta alongside the zucchini and drizzle with olive oil. Garnish with mint leaves and serve.

Note: *Feeley's roasted zucchini pairs incredibly well with a citrusy, lightly grassy Sauvignon Blanc, a grape variety that tends to bring out the character of fresh herbs.*

Sheamus Feeley
The Green Cart Deli

Fall to Your Knees Mac and Cheese

This recipe takes a little extra effort, but it is so worth it!

3½ cups elbow macaroni
1 ⅓ cups heavy cream
1 ⅓ cups half-and-half milk
⅔ cup sour cream
4 ounces cream cheese
1 egg
3 tablespoons flour
1 tablespoon Worcestershire sauce
1 teaspoon each garlic powder, onion powder, dry mustard and salt
¼ teaspoon cayenne pepper
⅛ teaspoon pepper
12 ounces Velveeta cheese, 1 inch cubes
15 ounces Gruyere cheese, shredded (can substitute Swiss)
1½ cups shredded Jack-and-Cheddar cheese
Pinch paprika

Preheat oven to 350°. Grease a 9x13-inch or deeper pan. Prepare macaroni according to package directions. Drain well and pour into baking pan. In a large mixing bowl, add heavy cream, half-and-half and sour cream. Break cream cheese into little pieces and add to bowl. Add egg, flour, Worcestershire, garlic powder, onion powder, dry mustard, cayenne pepper, salt and pepper. Combine very well with a wire whisk to break up cream cheese. It will look lumpy. Starting at corners of baking pan, place and push down Velveeta cubes. Work your way around and toward the middle pushing the cheese deep below the surface. Sprinkle Gruyere cheese evenly over top. Gently pour wet mixture over, covering all. Gently shake pan afterwards to settle liquid. Sprinkle Jack-and-Cheddar cheese over top. Sprinkle paprika on top of cheese. Bake approximately 30 minutes or until it starts to get brown and bubbly.

Sara Ray,
Sara's Dress Shop, Magnolia
Magnolia Blossom Festival & World Championship Steak Cook-Off®

Four Cheese Macaroni & Cheese

½ cup olive oil
1 medium onion, diced
2 cups elbow macaroni
4 cups milk
4 cups heavy whipping cream
2 tablespoons paprika
1 tablespoon pepper
1 tablespoon salt
1 cup cottage cheese
4 cups grated cheese (colby, Swiss, mozzarella and Parmesan),
    plus more for topping
Breadcrumbs for topping

In an oven-safe pan on top of the stove, cook onions in olive oil over medium heat until onions begin to carmelize. Cook macaroni al denté; drain. Add milk, cream, spices, cottage cheese and grated cheese. Stir noodle mixture into onions. Top with more cheese and breadcrumbs. Bake at 350° for 25 minutes or until golden brown on top.

The Ozark Cafe, Jasper
Buffalo River Elk Festival

Linguine with Tomato and Basil Sauce

4 large tomatoes, cubed
1 pound Brie cheese, torn
1 cup fresh basil, cut in strips
3 cloves garlic, minced
1 cup plus 1 tablespoon olive oil, divided
2½ teaspoons salt, divided
½ teaspoon pepper
1½ pounds linguine
Parmesan Cheese

Combine tomatoes, Brie cheese, basil, garlic, 1 cup olive oil, ½ teaspoon salt, and pepper. Let sit at least 2 hours at room temperature. Boil linguine with remaining oil and salt for about 8 to 10 minutes. Toss with sauce and serve immediately with Parmesan cheese.

Diane & Steve, Mountain Garden Getaway, Jasper
Cabins in the Ozarks

Italian Fettuccine

⅓ cup butter
⅓ cup flour
1 teaspoon salt
Dash white pepper
Dash freshly ground nutmeg
1 cup chicken broth
1 cup light cream
½ cup Romano or Parmesan cheese
1 cup grated aged cheese
1 pound fettuccine noodles, cooked

Melt butter; blend in flour and seasonings. Cook, stirring constantly, until bubbly. Add chicken broth and cream at one time, stirring until thickened and smooth. Add cheeses. Stir until cheese is melted. Pour over noodles.

Tontitown Grape Festival

Tontitown Grape Festival
August

St. Joseph's Parish
Tontitown
479.361.2615
www.tontitowngrapefestival.com

Tontitown is a small community located in Northwest Arkansas with a special pride for its humble beginnings. However, in August they gear up to share it with the world. The Tontitown Grape Festival began as a harvest celebration for a small group of Italian immigrants in 1898. After more than 113 years it has grown to include a large carnival, wine tasting, free nightly entertainment from Nashville recording artists, arts & crafts fair, grape stomp, and of course those Italian spaghetti dinners that have certainly become a famous ritual for thousands. The subsequent generations of these early settlers have not forgotten their heritage and they are happy to share it with anyone who attends. Buy locally grown grapes and you'll also want to try the grape ice cream! For a complete schedule, go to www.tontitowngrapefestival.com. There's something for everyone!

Fettuccine with Broccoli

¼ cup extra virgin olive oil
2½ cups fresh broccoli florets
3 large cloves garlic, minced
¼ teaspoon crushed red pepper
1 (9-ounce) package fettuccine pasta, cooked and drained
⅓ cup freshly grated Romano cheese

Over medium heat, cook broccoli, garlic and red pepper in oil. Cook, stirring frequently, until broccoli is tender. Add pasta and toss, coating well. Sprinkle with cheese and serve warm.

Pasta with Sage and Chocolate

1 pound spaghetti or fettuccine
8 tablespoons butter
4 shallots, finely minced
20 fresh ground sage leaves, plus more as garnish
Freshly ground black pepper or red pepper flakes
⅓ cup grated Parmigiano Reggiano cheese
1 to 2 ounces bittersweet chocolate, coarsely grated

Prepare pasta according to package directions; drain and reserve cooking water. Meanwhile, melt butter in a saucepan over medium heat and sauté shallots and sage leaves, about 8 minutes, until butter is golden brown. Toss pasta with sage-shallot butter and about ¼ cup pasta's cooking water. Season to taste with pepper. Serve topped with cheese and generous sprinkling of grated chocolate.

Eureka Springs Chocolate Lovers Festival

Scalloped Potatoes

1 cup chopped onion
2 cloves garlic, minced
¼ cup butter or margarine
¼ cup all-purpose flour
½ teaspoon salt
¼ teaspoon pepper
2½ cups milk
8 cups thinly sliced potatoes

For sauce, in a medium saucepan cook onion and garlic in hot butter until tender. Stir in flour, salt and pepper. Add milk all at once. Cook and stir over medium heat until thickened and bubbly. Remove from heat; set aside. Place ½ sliced potatoes in a greased 3-quart rectangular dish. Top with ½ sauce. Repeat layers. Bake, covered in a 350° oven 45 minutes. Uncover and bake 40 to 50 minutes more or until potatoes are tender. Let stand, uncovered for 10 minutes before serving.

Historic Oark General Store & Cafe

The Arkansas Derby

Held each April at Oak Lawn Park in Hot Springs, the Arkansas Derby is an exhilarating American Thoroughbred horse race. Beginning in 1936, this race has increased its profile and today attracts many of the best thoroughbreds in the country.

Scooter's Baked Potato

1 baking potato
2 tablespoons butter, melted
Kosher salt

Poke potato with fork. Roll in melted butter. Roll in kosher salt. Bake at 500° for 45 minutes. Delicious!!

"Scooters Restaurant" at The Hub, Marble Falls
Buffalo River Elk Festival

Seasoned Baked Potatoes

3 medium potatoes, peeled and thinly sliced
1 medium onion, thinly sliced
1 teaspoon dried basil or oregano
2 tablespoons melted butter
Salt and pepper, to taste

Preheat oven to 425°. Place ½ sliced potatoes and ½ sliced onions in a buttered 9-inch casserole dish. Sprinkle with ½ dried herbs and drizzle with 1 tablespoon butter. Repeat layers, ending with remaining melted butter. Season with salt and pepper, to taste. Cover and bake 20 minutes. Uncover and bake 15 to 20 minutes longer, or until potatoes are tender.

Angel Eggs

6 hard-cooked eggs, peeled and cut lengthwise
1 cup Miracle Whip
2 tablespoons sweet pickle relish
⅛ teaspoon salt
1 teaspoon ground black pepper
Paprika for garnish

Pop out (remove) the egg yolks to a small bowl and mash with a fork. Add Miracle Whip, pickle relish, salt and pepper; mix thoroughly. Fill empty egg white shells with mixture and sprinkle lightly with paprika. Cover lightly with plastic wrap and refrigerate up to 1 day before serving. The filling of this recipe is on the firm side. Add a tad more Miracle Whip if you would like it a bit softer. Delicious as a side dish or appetizer.

Vi Murray
Jacksonville Parks and Recreation

Jacksonville Parks and Recreation

Jacksonville • 501.982.0818 • www.jacksonvillesoars.com

The Jacksonville Parks and Recreation has been sponsoring a craft sale since the seventies. The first craft sale was named "Christmas Craft Sale" and was held at 201 West Martin Street, which at the time housed the Parks and Recreation Department. After several years, the Christmas Craft Sale was relocated to the Jacksonville Boys Club. In 1995, when the Jacksonville Community Center was built, the craft sale found its home. Despite changing names, locations and dates, the craft sale kept one concept consistent—all products must be hand-made. In 2008, the name was changed to the "Holiday Craft and Gift Sale." This annual event takes place at the Jacksonville Community Center and is held the weekend before Thanksgiving. Individuals requesting information for the Holiday Craft and Gift Sale can call 501.982.0818.

Wild Rice with Pecans

2 tablespoons butter or margarine
2 (6-ounce) packages long grain and wild rice mix
4 cups chicken broth
¼ cup chopped green onions
8 medium mushrooms, sliced
1½ cups chopped pecans, toasted

Melt butter in a large Dutch oven. Add rice and cook over medium heat, stirring frequently, until light brown. Stir in rice seasoning packets, broth, green onions and mushrooms. Bring to a boil and remove from heat. Pour into a lightly greased 3-quart baking dish. Bake, covered, at 350° for 15 minutes then stir will. Return to oven and bake another 15 minutes or until rice is tender and liquid is absorbed. Stir in pecans before serving.

Pine Bluff Convention and Visitors Bureau

Cossatot River

If you are an experienced canoeist, the Cossatot River beacons you. A watershed basin, this river is the perfect place for a white water challenge. After good rainfall, the water is high and gives way for class IV-V paddling, which is for experts only.

Cumin Rice

⅓ cup chopped onion
¼ cup chopped green bell pepper
1 cup uncooked rice
2 tablespoons bacon drippings or vegetable oil
2 cups beef broth or consommé
1 tablespoon Worcestershire sauce
¾ teaspoon salt
¾ teaspoon cumin seed

Cook onion, pepper and rice in bacon drippings until rice is golden brown. Use low heat and stir to prevent over-browning. While rice is cooking, bring beef broth to a boil. Turn rice, with drippings, into shallow 2-quart casserole. Add broth, Worcestershire sauce, salt and cumin; stir well. Cover tightly with lid or foil and bake at 350° for 30 minutes or until rice is tender and liquid is absorbed.

Rice Pilaf

2 tablespoons butter
1 small onion, chopped
1 cup uncooked long-grain rice
2 cups chicken broth
¼ teaspoon salt

Melt butter in 3-quart saucepan over medium heat. Add onion and cook until tender. Stir in rice and brown, stirring frequently. Stir in broth and salt; heat to a boil. Reduce heat and cover. Simmer 16 minutes. DO NOT OPEN COVER. Remove from heat. Allow to stand, covered, for 5 minutes.

Cheesy Green Chile Rice

4 cups uncooked rice
2 cups sour cream
Salt
2 cups grated Monterey Jack cheese
4 (4-ounce) cans chopped green chiles
Butter

Cook rice according to package directions. Preheat oven to 350°. Combine cooked rice with sour cream and season with salt to taste. In a buttered casserole dish, spread ½ rice mixture. Sprinkle with 1 cup cheese. Top with all the green chilies. Spread remaining rice on top of chilies, sprinkle with remaining cheese, and dot with butter. Bake 30 minutes.

Meat & Seafood

Slow-Cooked Turkey Sandwiches

This delicious recipe serves a crowd... easily.

6 cups cubed cooked turkey
2 cups cubed Velveeta
1 (10¾-ounce) can condensed cream of chicken soup
1 (10¾-ounce) can condensed cream of mushroom soup
½ cup finely chopped onion
½ cup chopped celery
22 small split wheat buns

Combine everything, except buns in a crockpot. Cover and cook on low for 3 to 4 hours. Toast buns. Give turkey mixture a good stir and spoon over buns.

Wildlife Farms

178 Wildlife Farms Lane • Casscoe
870.241.3275 • www.wildlifefarms.com

Nestled on the banks of the White River is a beautiful, rustic lodge, the centerpiece of Wildlife Farms. Offering prime duck, turkey, deer, dove, pheasant, and big game hunting, Wildlife Farms is one of the oldest hunting outfitters in Arkansas. The 1900 acre property boasts 5.5 miles of river frontage and contains flooded, old growth hardwood timber, oxbow lakes and cypress sloughs. The hunting guides at Wildlife Farms are seasoned huntsman and are experts on the land. In addition to hunting, Wildlife Farms also provides some of the best skeet shooting, sporting clays, and trap shooting facilities anywhere. This outdoorsman's paradise is backed by excellent lodging, meals, and service, making it a prime meeting place for corporate retreats. Visit our website to learn more about our hunts, see what's available for the family, view photos of the lodge and the grounds, and find out how Wildlife Farms can cater to your needs.

Chicken and Vegetables with Soy Dipping Sauce

4 boneless, skinless chicken breast halves
½ teaspoon salt
¼ teaspoon pepper
3 cups sliced asparagus
1 cup halved sugar snap peas
¼ cup chopped fresh cilantro
¼ cup soy sauce
2 tablespoons rice vinegar
2 tablespoons sweet rice wine
½ teaspoon dark sesame oil

Salt and pepper chicken and arrange in a large vegetable steamer. Add water to a large pan, about 1 inch deep, and bring to a boil. Place steamer in pan, cover and steam chicken 10 minutes, or until done. Add asparagus and peas to steamer, cover and cook 2 minutes, or until vegetables are tender. Whisk cilantro and remaining ingredients until mixed well. Serve over chicken and vegetables.

The Fouke Monster and the White River Monster

Every place needs a mystery, and Arkansas has plenty! The Fouke Monster and the White River Monster are the stuff of legends, and each new eye-witness account revives the mystery. The Fouke Monster is reported to be six feet tall and hairy, and the White River Monster is allegedly sea-serpent-like and 30 feet long. Keep an eye out for these unexplained monsters… Who knows, you just might have a tale to tell of your own!

Baked Chicken and Yellow Rice

4 to 5 chicken breasts
Salt to taste
½ cup (more or less) self-rising flour
2 to 3 tablespoons oil
1 box yellow rice
1 (10¾-ounce) can cream of mushroom soup
1 soup can water

Rinse chicken and pat dry. Salt and flour chicken. Pour oil into baking pan; place chicken in pan. Bake at 350° for 45 minutes; drain. Prepare rice according to package directions. Place rice around chicken breasts. Combine soup and water; pour over chicken and rice. Return to oven and bake another 45 minutes to 1 hour or until chicken is tender and golden brown.

Ginger Chicken

1½ pounds chicken breasts
Garlic salt
Pepper
½ cup flour
½ cup breadcrumbs
2 tablespoons sugar
2 tablespoons soy sauce
1 tablespoon grated fresh ginger

Cut chicken breasts into 1-inch squares. Season with garlic salt and pepper. Coat with flour and breadcrumbs. Deep fry until golden brown. Combine sugar, soy sauce and fresh ginger. Coat chicken with sauce and serve.

Dennis & Naomi Gundersen, owners
Big Oak Cabin, Jasper
Cabins in the Ozarks

Cabins in the Ozarks

2½ Miles North of Jasper, on Scenic Byway 7
870.446.2693 • www.cabinsintheozarks.net

Welcome to Newton County, Arkansas, where tranquility is abundant! Cabins in the Ozarks offers a variety of accommodations and amenities to suit your needs — from cozy cottages that sleep 2, to colossal cabins that sleep 12 with game rooms and hot tubs — all centrally located in the county. You will find caves, creeks, cliffs, rivers, scenic overlooks, swimming holes, waterfalls and wildlife! Enjoy scenic drives, canoeing, fishing, hiking, horseback riding, motorcycling or rock climbing adventures that could keep you entertained for weeks. Throughout the year you might catch a fair or festival, parade or rodeo, spring or fall color tour, rock climbing or hiking event, an artist tour with live demonstrations, plus much more. Visit our website at www.cabinsintheozarks.net or call 800-669-3762 or 870-446-2810.

In the heart of Newton County & the Buffalo National River

(870) 446-2810 • (800) 669-3762
www.cabinsintheozarks.net

"Cabins with Hot Tubs & Game Rooms or Cozy Cottages for Two"

Easy Baked Chicken Breasts

8 chicken breast halves, skinned and boned
4 (4x4-inch) slices Swiss cheese
1 (10.5-ounce) can cream of chicken soup
¼ cup dry white wine
1 cup herb-seasoned stuffing mix
2 tablespoons butter, melted

Arrange chicken in lightly greased 8x12-inch baking dish. Top with cheese slices. Combine soup and wine; stir well. Spoon sauce over chicken. Crush stuffing mix, sprinkle over chicken, drizzle with butter, bake at 350° for 45 minutes. Serves 8.

Hot Springs Arts & and Crafts Fair

Veggie Chicken Wraps

1 (8-ounce) carton spreadable garden vegetable cream cheese
4 (8-inch) flour tortillas
2 cups shredded romaine
2 small tomatoes, thinly sliced
8 slices provolone cheese
1 small red onion, thinly sliced
2 cups diced cooked chicken

Spread cream cheese evenly over each tortilla. Layer with romaine, tomatoes, cheese, onion and chicken. Roll up tightly. Cut wraps in half to serve.

Oil Town Festival

Peppery Chicken Wings

16 chicken wings (about 2 pounds)
1 teaspoon peanut or vegetable oil
1 teaspoon cayenne pepper
½ cup plain low-fat yogurt
¼ cup buttermilk
½ cup crumbled blue cheese (1 ounce)
½ small yellow onion, grated
1 teaspoon cider vinegar

Preheat broiler. Separate chicken wings at joint; remove and discard wing tips. In a medium-size bowl, combine oil and cayenne pepper. Add chicken and turn until well coated. Place chicken wings on broiler pan rack and broil about 8 inches from heat, turning occasionally, until crisp and golden, about 20 minutes. Meanwhile, prepare dip. In medium-size bowl, whisk yogurt, buttermilk, blue cheese, onion and vinegar. Transfer to small serving bowl and set in center of a large round platter and arrange broiled chicken wings around it. Serves 8.

Betty Harvey, Little Rock Farmers' Market
Jane and Elaine's Plants and Produce

Chicken Breasts Greek Style

This is a great dish! Serve with Caesar salad or Greek Salad.

6 boneless, skinless chicken breast halves
1 package frozen chopped spinach, thawed
1 (4-ounce) package feta cheese, crumbled
½ cup mayonnaise
1 clove garlic, minced
¼ cup flour
½ teaspoon paprika
12 strips bacon
Salt
Pepper

Wash chicken breasts under cold running water and set aside. Drain and squeeze liquid from spinach. Combine with Feta cheese, mayonnaise and garlic. Cut pockets into chicken breasts, stuff mixture into cuts. Combine flour and paprika, then coat stuffed chicken breasts. Wrap 2 strips bacon around each breast and place on baking rack in baking dish. Bake uncovered at 325° for 1 hour or until done.

Alice Chambers
Greers Ferry Lake/Little Red River Shoreline Cleanup

Nelson Kabobs

This makes a great appetizer or party finger food.

1 pound chicken tenders, cut into cubes
1 pound smoked sausage, cut into cubes
(with cheese is best)
60 to 70 count cooked shrimp,
peeled, deveined and tails removed
1 large purple onion
1 bell pepper

Place each item on skewer alternating meats and vegetables. You will want at least 2 but no more than 3 of each meat on a skewer. Sprinkle with Cavender's Greek seasoning and grill until chicken is done being careful not to burn the onion.

David Nelson, Steak Cook-off Chairman
Magnolia Blossom Festival & World Championship Steak Cook-Off®

Shrimp and Grits

2 bacon slices
1 pound medium-size raw shrimp,
    peeled and deveined
⅛ teaspoon salt
¼ teaspoon pepper
¼ cup all-purpose flour
1 cup sliced fresh mushrooms

2 teaspoons canola oil
½ cup chopped green onions
2 garlic cloves, minced
1 cup chicken broth
2 tablespoons fresh lemon juice
¼ teaspoon hot sauce
Cheese grits

Cook bacon in a large nonstick skillet until crisp. Remove bacon to drain on paper towels, reserving 1 teaspoon drippings in skillet. Sprinkle shrimp with salt and pepper; dredge in flour. Sauté mushrooms in hot drippings with oil 5 minutes or until tender. Add green onions and sauté 2 minutes. Add shrimp and garlic. Sauté 2 minutes or until shrimp are lightly browned. Stir in chicken broth, lemon juice and hot sauce. Cook 2 more minutes, stirring to loosen particles from bottom of skillet. Spoon shrimp mixture over hot cheese grits. Crumble bacon over top. Serves 4 to 6.

Steamboat Festival Days
First Weekend in June

Downtown, on the banks of the White River
DesArc
870.256.5289
www.steamboatdays.net

For over 26 years, the first week in June belongs to Steamboat Days! The festivities are kicked off with a gospel concert on Wednesday, the Miss Steamboat Days pageant is held on Thursday, and Friday gets the whole event into high gear with a street dance that grooves until midnight. Bright and early at 6:00 a.m. on Saturday the bass tournament is held on the White River. Are motorcycles more your thing than bass fishing? Then at 10:00 a.m. make your way to the 50-mile poker run. The children's activities are from 10:00 — 12:00, and then it's time to shop, when the vendors go live. The day winds down with the Grand Ole Opry at 8:00 and fireworks at 11:00.

Jambalaya

½ cup oil
1 chicken, cut up and deboned (can use chicken breasts)
1½ pounds Andouille/smoked sausage, cut in ½-inch slices
4 cups chopped onions
2 cups chopped celery
2 cups chopped green bell peppers
1 tablespoon chopped garlic
5 cups chicken broth
1 (14-ounce) can stewed tomatoes
2 heaping teaspoons salt
1½ teaspoons cayenne pepper
1 teaspoon thyme
¼ teaspoon oregano
4 cups rice
1 to 2 tablespoons Kitchen Bouquet
1 cup chopped green onions
1 pound precooked shrimp

Season and brown chicken in oil over medium-high heat. Add sausage to pot and sauté with chicken. Remove both from pot. Sauté onions, celery, green peppers and garlic to desired tenderness. Return chicken and sausage to pot. Add broth, stewed tomatoes and spices; bring to a boil. Add rice and return to a boil. Cover with a tight lid and reduce heat to simmer. Cook 10 minutes; remove cover and quickly turn rice from top to bottom completely. Cook 15 minutes; add green onions. Add green onions; cook 5 minutes. Add shrimp when rice is finished to avoid overcooking shrimp. Makes 12 servings.

Parker Homestead Festival

Pecan Crusted Chilean Sea Bass

4 (6-ounce) Chilean sea bass filets
½ pound unsalted butter, softened
½ cup chopped pecans
¼ cup fresh shredded Parmesan cheese
Zest of 1 lemon
Kosher salt and freshly ground black pepper, to taste

Combine butter, pecans, cheese, lemon, salt and pepper; chill. Sear sea bass on each side in cast iron skillet on high heat. Generously apply pecan crust to each filet. Place in 425° oven for 10 minutes. Enjoy immediately!

Postmasters Grill

Postmasters Grill

Camden • 870.574.0374 • www.postmastersgrill.com

Listed on the National Register of Historic Places and located in the heart of downtown Camden, the old Camden Post office was completed in 1896. Many people of the time proclaimed that Camden (population 5,000) was probably the smallest town in the United States with a federal government building. In the early 70's the building was scheduled to be demolished, but was saved, and recently sold in 2010. After an 18 month long renovation and restoration, the Old Camden Post Office has been reborn as Postmasters Grill. The restaurant has an amazing selection of tantalizing  appetizers, salads, and extraordinary contemporary American Cuisine. Our chef's focus is on bringing you only the finest and freshest ingredients. Postmasters Grill is the perfect spot for a romantic evening, business engagement or a relaxed dinner in our dining room, bar or garden. Check out our website for current menu and events.

Seafood Lasagna

2 (1.8-ounce) packages white sauce mix
4 cups milk
1 teaspoon dried basil leaves
½ teaspoon dried thyme leaves
½ teaspoon garlic powder
¾ cup grated Parmesan cheese, divided
3 tablespoons Frank's Original Red Hot Cayenne Pepper Sauce
9 oven-ready lasagna pasta sheets
2 (10-ounce) packages chopped spinach, thawed & squeezed dry
1 pound cooked shrimp, peeled
1 pound flaked imitation crabmeat
2 cups shredded mozzarella, divided

Preheat oven to 400°. Prepare white sauce according to package directions, using milk and adding basil, thyme, and garlic powder. Stir in ½ cup Parmesan cheese and hot sauce. Spread 1 cup sauce in greased 9x13-inch pan. Layer 3 sheets crosswise over sauce. Do not let edges touch. Layer ½ seafood and spinach over pasta. Spoon 1 cup sauce over seafood. Sprinkle ¾ cup mozzarella cheese. Repeat layers a second time. Top with remaining pasta sheets, remaining sauce and cheeses. Cover pan with greased foil. Bake 40 minutes at 400°. Remove foil, bake 10 minutes or until top is brown and pasta is fully cooked. Let stand 15 minutes before serving.

Jennifer Rackley
Jacksonville Parks and Recreation

Crawfish Étouffée

1 stick butter
1 yellow onion, chopped
1 green bell pepper, chopped
1 cup chopped celery
2 garlic cloves, minced
1 bay leaf
¼ teaspoon thyme
1 teaspoon basil
1 pound crawfish tails
Creole seasoning, to taste
Tabasco hot sauce, to taste
1 can cream of mushroom soup
1 bunch green onions
¼ cup chopped parsley

Melt butter in large Dutch oven over medium-high heat. Sauté onion, bell pepper, celery and garlic until tender. Add seasonings and crawfish; cook 10 minutes. Add soup, ½ can water, green onions and parsley. Cook on low heat 30 minutes. Stir often to prevent sticking. Serve over rice.

King Biscuit Blues Festival

Haw Creek Falls

If in the mood for a quiet, relaxing time in the outdoors, Haw Creek Falls should be on the radar. Located within the Bayou Ranger District, Haw Creek Falls is on a small mountain creek with quaint falls, rocks and bluff.

Arkansas Crawfish Boil

Boiling Crawfish is like cooking Bar-B-Q, everybody does it different and every recipe is good!

1 sack (about 33 pounds) live crawfish
3 to 4 pounds red potatoes or small new potatoes
8 to 10 ears corn, shucked and thawed
2 pounds Cajun sausage, bite size pieces
2 (2-pound) bags Delta Donnie's Crawfish & Shrimp Boil
1 (80-quart) boiling pot with basket and lid
Propane jet burner
Stirring paddle
10 pounds ice

If crawfish are unwashed put in container and wash with cold water and remove any straw or bait. (DO NOT USE SALT.) Set aside. Fill pot with enough water to cover corn and potatoes and bring to boil. Put potatoes and corn in basket and place in boiling water, bring back to boil, cover and boil 10 minutes. Remove and put in clean cooler, cover and set aside. Place crawfish in basket. Add enough water to cover crawfish and bring back to boil, add 4 pounds seasoning and stir in with paddle to dissolve and immediately add crawfish. With HIGHEST HEAT POSSIBLE bring back to boil, stir and boil 3 to 5 minutes until crawfish are bright red and floating to top of pot. Add sausage to pot with crawfish. Return corn and potatoes to pot with crawfish and stir 2 minutes. Turn off heat and put 10 pounds ice in top of pot (do not stir) and cover. Let soak 20 minutes and serve. Ice will cause crawfish to sink to bottom of pot and absorb seasoning, the longer they soak the spicier they will be! Serves 8 to 10.

Delta Crawfish Market & Cafe

Smoked Sausage in a Skillet

1 pound smoked sausage, cut in rounds
1 large onion, cut in strips
1 large green bell pepper, cut in strips
1 tablespoon oil
1 can stewed tomatoes
1 tablespoon soy sauce
1 tablespoon Worcestershire sauce

Brown sausage, onions and peppers in oil. Add remaining ingredients and simmer until onions and peppers are tender. Serve over rice.

Sausage Stroganoff

1 garlic clove
2 pounds sausage
3 tablespoon flour
2 cups milk
2 large onions, chopped
2 (4-ounce) cans mushrooms
4 tablespoons butter
2 teaspoons soy sauce
2 tablespoons Worcestershire
Salt, pepper and paprika to taste
1 pint sour cream

Rub large skillet with garlic and heat. Brown sausage well. Pour off grease as it accumulates. Dredge sausage with flour and return to pan. Add milk and simmer until slightly thickened. Set aside. In a separate skillet, sauté onions and mushrooms in butte; add to sausage along with soy sauce, Worcestershire and seasonings. When mixture bubbles, add sour cream. Keep hot in chafing dish. Heap upon biscuits or pastry shells or use as a dip with Melba toast. Wonderful served in chafing dish for parties, large or small. For 50 or more people, double the recipe. When doubling, add only 3 onions. May be made in advance and frozen, eliminating sour cream. On day of party, thaw and heat in electric skillet, adding sour cream as called for in recipe.

Mrs. E.J. Hosey (Merrie Jack)
King Biscuit Blues Festival

Crowd Pleasin' Hot Tamale Pie

This is one of those fast and easy dishes where someone is typically hanging out beside the empty casserole dish to get the recipe. It's exceptionally delicious made with leftover chili from Russellville's Downtown Fall Festival & Chili Cook-off.

2 cans hot tamales, cut into bite-size pieces
1 can chili with beans
1 can whole-kernel corn, drained
1 cup chopped onion (yellow, white or green), divided
1 cup grated cheese (Cheddar, Monterey Jack or cheese of your choice)
½ cup chopped olives (green or black)

In a 9x13-inch casserole dish combine first 3 ingredients and ½ cup chopped onion. Top with grated cheese, remaining chopped onion and chopped olives. Heat in a 350° oven until hot and bubbly. Serve with crackers or cornbread and a fresh green or fruit salad.

Main Street Russellville
Taste of the Valley and Downtown Fall Festival & Chili Cook-off

Main Street Russellville

**320 West C Street @ The Depot,
in the heart of Downtown Russellville
479.967.1437
www.mainstreetrussellville.com**

Located just off of Interstate 40 halfway between Little Rock and Fort Smith you'll find the Pope County seat of Russellville, Arkansas. The historic heart of the city comes together at the crossroads of Highway 7 & 64, and since 1992 Main Street Russellville has been dedicated to the mission of revitalizing and redeveloping the traditional central business district within the context of historic preservation. Design, technical and grant assistance has resulted in many rehabilitated buildings as well as the restoration of the historic Missouri-Pacific Depot as a local landmark. In addition, Main Street Russellville sponsors many community trademark events that include the Downtown Fall Festival & Chili Cook-off on the last Saturday of each October, and the award-winning Taste of the Valley held on the last Thursday each April. These are just two of the events that help Main Street Russellville fulfill its mission by bringing people back downtown. Contact Main Street Russellville to find out more about events and opportunities in Russellville's historic downtown district.

Just Good Tamale Pie

1 pound ground beef
1 small onion, chopped
½ teaspoon garlic salt
1 (10-ounce) can Rotel
1 (12-ounce) can whole-kernel corn, drained
1 (15-ounce) can ranch-style pinto beans
1 (15-ounce) can Spanish rice
1 (9-ounce) bag Doritos
Velveeta Cheese

Brown ground beef, onion and garlic salt. Drain fat. Stir in Rotel tomatoes, corn, beans and rice. Cook 10 minutes and pour into baking dish. Blend in chips and top with sliced Velveeta. Bake at 450° until cheese bubbles.

Eloise Oliver
BPW Barn Sale

Beef & Cheese Enchiladas

1 pound ground beef
1 large onion, finely chopped
2 garlic cloves, finely chopped
1 package instant brown gravy mix
½ cup chicken broth
1 tablespoon ground red chiles
1 tablespoon ground cumin
1 teaspoon dried oregano leaves
1 can chopped tomatoes
2 cans tomato sauce
12 corn (or flour) tortillas
1 pound shredded Cheddar cheese

Brown beef and drain off excess grease. Add onion and garlic; cook until tender. Set aside. In a 2-quart pan, combine gravy mix, chicken broth and spices. Bring to a boil and stir in tomatoes and tomato sauce. Simmer 10 minutes. While that is simmering, preheat oven to 350°. Dip each tortilla into sauce to coat both sides. Spoon about 3 tablespoons meat and 2 tablespoons cheese in center of each tortilla. Roll up and place seam-side-down in a greased 9x13-inch baking dish. Pour remaining sauce over top and sprinkle with remaining cheese. Bake, uncovered, 15 to 20 minutes or until heated thoroughly.

Crockpot Lasagna

¾ pound Italian sausage
1 tablespoon minced onion
1¼ pounds hamburger
1½ jars Bertolli Tomato Basil Spaghetti Sauce
2 teaspoons Italian seasoning
½ teaspoon oregano
¼ teaspoon thyme
1 (15-ounce) container part-skim ricotta cheese
1 cup shredded Parmesan cheese
3 cups shredded mozzarella cheese, divided
12 uncooked lasagna noodles

Spray crockpot with nonstick cooking spray. In large skillet, cook sausage and onion over medium heat until sausage is no longer pink. Drain and remove to bowl. In same skillet, brown hamburger. Add sausage back to skillet. Add sauce and seasonings; mix well. Reduce heat to low. In a bowl, combine ricotta, Parmesan and 2 cups mozzarella. Spoon ¼ sausage mixture into crockpot and top with 4 noodles broken to fit. Top with ½ cheese mixture, then ¼ sausage mixture and 4 noodles. Make another layer of cheese, sausage, and noodles, then finish with remaining sausage mixture. Cover and cook on low 6 hours or high 3 to 4 hours. Sprinkle with remaining mozzarella cheese, cover and cook 15 minutes or until cheese is melted.

Bella Vista Arts and Crafts Fair

Johnny Marzetti

1½ pounds ground beef
Salt and pepper to taste
12 ounces shredded Cheddar cheese
1 medium onion
1 small can mushrooms
4 cups cooked macaroni
1 (8-ounce) can tomato sauce
1 (4-ounce) can tomato sauce

Brown ground beef and onions. Salt and pepper to taste. Mix in ½ cheese and larger can tomato sauce. Spread cooked macaroni in oblong baking dish. Pour meat and cheese mixture over macaroni. Top with smaller can tomato sauce and remaining cheese. Bake at 350° until hot and bubbly. Serves 8.

Rock 'n Roll Highway 67 Music Festival

Rock and Roll Highway 67 Music Festival
First Weekend in October

Downtown Pocahontas
870.892.0254
www.seerandolphcounty.com

The Annual Rock and Roll Highway 67 Music Festival is held each year in Pocahontas, Arkansas, along the historic Rock and Roll Highway 67 where many of the early stars of rock played at various venues. This is 1950's nostalgia all the way! Come cruise the strip, take a historic music tour, do the twist at the sock hop, show off your hula hoop skills, shop till you drop with vendors of all types, and enjoy two days and nights of music from the generation that gave birth to Rock 'n Roll. You never know what famous Rock and Roll headliner will perform during the final evening's concert. Call 870.892.0254 or go to SeeRandolphCounty.com for more information.

House 3-Meat Loaf

1 pound each ground Elk, Buffalo and Wild Razorback
1½ cups chopped onion
1 green bell pepper, chopped
1 tomato, chopped
3 garlic cloves
3 eggs, beaten
½ cup cream
1 cup rolled oats
1 cup Parmesan cheese
1½ teaspoons salt
1 teaspoon black pepper
½ cup ketchup

Preheat oven to 350°. Mix all ingredients, except ketchup, with hands until well blended. Form into loaf on well-oiled cookie sheet. Baste loaf with ketchup. Bake 1½ hours. Cool 15 minutes before slicing.

The Arkansas House & Boardwalk Café Arkansas, Jasper
Buffalo River Elk Festival

Myrtie Mae's Meatloaf

2½ pounds ground beef
⅓ cup croutons
1 large yellow onion, diced
1 large egg, slightly beaten
⅔ teaspoon salt
¼ teaspoon black pepper
12 ounces (about 1½ cups) ketchup
⅓ cup brown sugar
1¼ teaspoon Dijon mustard

Mix beef, croutons, onions, egg, salt and pepper; form into a loaf. Whisk ketchup, brown sugar and mustard together and pour over loaf. Bake at 300° for 45 to 60 minutes. Serves 8 to 10.

VW Festival, Swap Meet & Tourcade

Swedish Meatballs

1 cup breadcrumbs
⅓ cup milk
1 pound ground beef
1 egg, beaten
⅓ cup chopped onions
½ teaspoon nutmeg
Salt and pepper to taste
2 tablespoons margarine
2 tablespoons flour
1 beef buillon cube
½ cup light cream

Soak bread crumbs in milk; mix well with ground beef, egg, onions, nutmeg, salt and pepper. Form into 1 inch balls and brown in 2 tablespoons margarine. Remove meatballs. Add flour, buillon cube, cream and 1 cup hot water to grease in pan. Stir until thickens. Add meatballs and simmer 15 minutes.

Wildflower Bed & Breakfast on the Square

Gourmet Meatloaf

Filling:

1 cup fresh mushrooms, sliced (or canned sliced mushrooms)
½ cup chopped onions
2 tablespoons butter
⅓ cup sour cream

Meatloaf:

1½ pounds lean ground beef
¾ cut uncooked oats
1 egg, beaten
2 teaspoons salt (optional or to taste)
¼ teaspoon pepper
1 tablespoon Worcestershire sauce
⅔ cup milk

Preheat oven to 350°. For filling, lightly brown mushrooms and onions in butter. Remove from heat and stir in sour cream. Set aside. For meatloaf, combine all ingredients. Place half of meat mixture in pan. Make a well for filling. Spoon filling into well. Shape remainder of meat mixture over filling and seal. Bake 1 hour. Let stand 5 minutes before cutting. Serve with rice or your favorite potatoes.

Mt. Magazine International Butterfly Festival

Chicken Fried Steak

3 to 4 tablespoons shortening
1 top round steak, tenderized
2 to 3 tablespoons all-purpose flour, plus extra for dusting
Salt, pepper, Lawry's seasoned salt and garlic salt
Milk

Place shortening in a cast-iron frying pan. Cut steak into 2 or 3 pieces and dust with flour and seasonings to taste. When grease is hot, add steak and cook until brown on both sides. Remove steak and make gravy by adding 2 or 3 tablespoons flour to grease and steak residue in pan. Stir until well mixed. Add milk (amount depends on whether you like your gravy thick or thin). Continue stirring so gravy won't be lumpy. When desired consistency is reached, add steak and continue to boil 1 or 2 minutes. Now it's ready to serve.

Patty Walker
Jacksonville Parks and Recreation

Fall Foilage

There are many places in the United States to witness fall foliage, and Arkansas is at the top of the list. Boasting extraordinary scenic drives of amazing fall colors, there are three primary areas for taking in nature's majesty. Area One is the Ozark Mountain region, which begins in late September goes through early October, with the peak in late October. In early October, within a week or so following the Ozark Mountain region, the Ouachitas and Arkansas River Valley begin to turn, and this is Area Two. Early November is normally the peak time for this area. Last but certainly not least is Area Three, which includes the Delta (east) and Gulf Coastal Plain (south). Both are usually transformed by early to mid-November.

World Championship Steak Cook-Off® Marinade

Three time winning recipes – 1999, 2000, and 2002.

1¼-inch thick ribeye steaks
Adolph's Meat Tenderizer with Spices
Bodacious Bar B Que Spices
Crisco vegetable oil

Sprinkle Adolph's Meat Tenderizer with Spices on steak and rub evenly. Liberally sprinkle Bodacious Bar B Que Spices on the steak and rub evenly. Lightly pour Crisco Vegetable Oil on the steak and rub evenly. Flip steaks over and repeat the entire marinade process. Let marinate in the refrigerator for 4 hours. Bring to room temperature for 30 minutes before cooking. Cook steaks to desired doneness over a 300° to 350° charcoal fire. World Championship Steak Cook-Off® steaks are judged based on medium doneness (pink line in the center).

Farmers Bank and Trust Team
Scott White, Chief Cook
Magnolia Blossom Festival & World Championship Steak Cook-Off®

Miss Laura's Bordello

Miss Laura's was one of 7 Bordellos located on "The Row" in 1900. The red-light district was on Front Street; Laura Zeiglar came from Vermont, had the building constructed and opened for business in 1903. The first brothel to be placed on the National Register, it has been the official Visitor Center for Fort Smith since 1992.

Bar-B-Que Brisket

1 whole brisket
1 tablespoon liquid smoke,
    plus more for soaking over night
Hickory salt
⅔ cup ketchup
1 tablespoon sugar
1 tablespoon Worcestershire sauce
1 tablespoon vinegar
Dash chili powder

Remove all fat and bone from brisket. Sprinkle with liquid smoke and refrigerate over night. Before cooking, sprinkle with hickory salt. Roll it up to fit into crockpot. Cook 6 to 8 hours in crockpot (or 1 hour per pound in 300° oven). To make barbecue sauce, combine ketchup, sugar, Worcstershire, vinegar, 1 tablespoon liquid smoke and chili powder. Slice thin and serve with barbecue sauce.

Fort Smith Convention & Visitors Bureau

Family Dinner Roast

Beef Roast (rump, shoulder or arm roast)
Garlic, sliced (to taste)
1 cup red wine
½ cup flour
2 to 3 packages brown gravy mix
Salt

Cut slits in meat and insert garlic to taste. Place in pan and add water to cover ¾ of the way. Add red wine, pouring it over meat. Cover with foil and cook at 350° until desired doneness. Check occasionally to see if more water is needed. For gravy, remove meat and pour off juices into a saucepan. Bring to a boil. Meanwhile, combine about ½ cup flour with brown gravy mix; add water per gravy package directions. Mix well, removing all lumps. Add to drippings and continue to cook, stirring constantly, until slightly thickened. Add salt to taste and more water if needed. For our large family gatherings, we cook 10 to 12 pounds meat (3 or 4 roasts) in a large roaster using about 2 cups wine and 4 to 6 cups water.

Altus Grape Festival

Altus Grape Festival
Last weekend in July

Altus City Park
479.468.4684
www.altusgrapefest.com

Since 1984, the Altus Grape Festival has celebrated the success of our past and present grape growers. Held in Altus City Park, the events are fun for the entire family. The celebrity and public grape stomps, free wine tasting, and live music are traditional favorites, occurring year after year. Food vendors of all types and arts and crafts booths fill the park. But don't forget there's the Blessing of the Harvest, the Vine Cutting Ceremony, and tours of the local wineries. The citizens of Altus are ready to make this a pleasurable experience to all who attend, and the best part is the admission is FREE!

Venison Roast

4 pounds venison roast
2 heaping tablespoons bacon/sausage grease
1 package Lipton onion soup mix
1 can cream of mushroom soup
20 baby carrots
5 red potatoes, peeled and quartered
5 purple onions, peeled and quartered

Preheat oven to 300°. In a large Dutch oven, brown roast in grease over medium-high heat. Remove roast, set aside. Add onion soup, 4 cups water and soup to Dutch oven; stir thoroughly. Return roast to Dutch oven and cover. Bake at 300° for 3 hours. Add baby carrots and potatoes and bake another 30 minutes. Add onions and bake another 30 minutes. Serve and enjoy!

Charlie Campbell, Father-in-Law Extraordinaire

Arkansas Big Buck Classic
Fourth Weekend in January

Arkansas State Fairgrounds
Little Rock
501.985.1533
www.bigbuckclassic.com

Fall is what whitetail hunters live for in Arkansas! Cooler weather...football games...and deer hunting! But January is when they all get together in one weekend at one place to celebrate another Arkansas Tradition, The Arkansas Big Buck Classic! Held the fourth weekend of January each year since 1990, The Arkansas Big Buck Classic is one of the largest hunting trade shows in the country. The Arkansas State Fairgrounds is transformed that weekend into an entire event place for not just whitetail hunters but outdoors enthusiasts of all types and ages. It is entertainment for the whole family with rock climbing, rattlesnake handling, live animals, deer scoring, bow fishing, vendors selling wares, great food and more! You do not want to miss it!

Cream Cheese Stuffed Pork Loin

1 pork loin
Cavender's Greek Seasoning
4 to 5 serrano peppers
1 onion, chopped
3 (8-ounce) packages cream cheese, softened
1 pound bacon
1 box round toothpicks

Butterfly cut pork loin, fold open and cover inside and out with Cavender's; set aside. Slice peppers lengthwise, remove seeds and chop into small pieces. Combine with onion and cream cheese. Stuff mixture into pork loin. Wrap with bacon using toothpicks to hold bacon in place and to keep pork loin closed as tight as possible. Be sure to count your toothpicks so you will know how many you have to pull out when the cooking is done. Wrap pork loin in foil (make sure it is completely sealed). Cook in Dutch oven 3 to 4 hours at 350°. Drain juices, slice and enjoy.

Backwoods Bakers, Fayetteville, 1st place 2009 Main Dish winner
Buffalo River Elk Festival

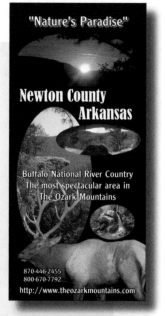

Buffalo River Elk Festival
Late June

The Courthouse Square
Jasper
870.446.2455 or 870.446.2693
www.theozarkmountains.com

Make plans to attend the Buffalo River Elk Festival in Jasper. Held annually, this late June event celebrates the return of elk to Newton County. The Courthouse Square features the talents of many artists and crafters, while streets off the square continue with wildlife exhibits, musical entertainment, and activities for kids of all ages. Although, the Kid's Fishing Derby, Arkansas Elk Calling Contest, Miss Elk Fest Pageant, and the Elk Permit Drawings are main attractions, Arkansas' Premier Dutch Oven Cook-Off has become the must-see event of the Festival. Contestants set up their camps, dress old-west style and cook some very tasty dishes in Dutch ovens, over hot coals, just like they did in the 1800's. Once the judging is complete and the winners are announced, you'll enjoy sampling the vittles they've prepared. The festival ends on Saturday night with a brilliant fireworks display.

Golden Ham Haystacks

1 can sliced pineapple
4 slices rye bread
2 tablespoons spreadable butter
½ teaspoon dry mustard
4 slices high-quality cooked ham, sliced ¼-inch thick
4 slices American cheese
Paprika
1 cup shoestring potatoes

Preheat oven to 400°. Drain pineapple and spread on paper towels to dry. Toast bread. Mix butter and dry mustard and spread on one side of each toasted slice. Place buttered side up on cookie sheet. Place 1 slice ham, 1 slice cheese and 1 slice pineapple on each slice of toast and sprinkle with paprika. Place several shoestring potatoes in top. Bake 10 to 12 minutes or until cheese melts.

Newton County

"NATURE'S PARADISE" is Newton County, Arkansas! The most spectacular area in the Ozark Mountains and Buffalo National River Country, it is the place to be for recreation, relaxation & reflection. Proclaimed the "Elk Capital of Arkansas" in 1998, Newton County offers everything for the day tripper, vacationer and nature lover. The Buffalo National River, with its many waterfalls, caves, swimming & fishing holes, caters to hikers, canoeist, fishermen and birders alike. Whether you have a car, motorcycle or mountain bike, a leisurely drive thru Newton County will find rolling terrain, fantastic overlooks, and nature at its best. www.theozarkmountains.com

Mexicali Pork Chop Casserole

1 tablespoon unsalted margarine
1 large yellow onion, halved and sliced thin
1 medium sweet green pepper, cored seeded and cut into 1-inch squares
1 medium sweet red pepper, cored seeded and cut into 1-inch squares
1 can low-sodium tomatoes, drained and chopped
1 cup frozen whole-kernel corn, thawed and drained
1 teaspoon dried marjoram
4 lean rib pork chops (about 1 pound), trimmed of fat

Preheat oven to 350°. Melt margarine in heavy 10-inch skillet over moderate heat. Add onion, green and red pepper; cook uncovered about 5 minutes. Add tomatoes, corn and marjoram. Raise heat to high and cook uncovered 5 minutes longer. Transfer to an ungreased shallow casserole or 9-inch pie pan. In same skillet, over moderate heat, cook pork chops 2 minutes on each side. Lay chops on top of vegetable mixture. Cover with aluminum foil and bake 12 to 15 minutes or until the pork chops are done. Serves 4.

Betty Harvey, Little Rock Farmers' Market
Jane and Elaine's Plants and Produce

Parmesan Breaded Pork Chops

1 cup seasoned breadcrumbs
3 tablespoons grated Parmesan cheese
Salt and pepper to taste
1 egg
2 tablespoons milk
8 pork chops
½ tablespoon butter

Mix breadcrumbs, cheese, salt and pepper in a shallow dish. Beat egg and milk in a separate shallow dish. Dip pork into crumb mixture, into egg mixture and again into crumb mixture to coat. Melt butter in a baking dish. Lay pork chops in a single layer in dish. Bake at 325° for 1 hour, turning after 30 minutes, or until brown and cooked through. Serves 4 to 8.

Junior League of Pine Bluff
Pine Bluff Convention and Visitors Bureau

Peach and Bourbon Marinade

This marinade best compliments pork.

4 fresh peaches, pitted
1 cup bourbon
3 stalks green onions, roots removed
1 tablespoon Sambal Oelek (chili paste)
3 tablespoons brown sugar
2 sprigs parsley
2 sprigs cilantro

Place all ingredients in a blender and blend until smooth. Pour over meat of your choice.

Winthrop Rockefeller Institute Saturday Chef's Series

Peach BBQ

5 strips bacon
Yellow onion
1 small can tomato paste
1 recipe Peach and Bourbon Marinade

Heat a medium-sized pot to medium heat and cook bacon to render fat. Add onion and cook until lightly brown. Add tomato paste and caramelize. Add marinade, bring to a boil, and cook 5 minutes. Add mixture to blender and pureé until smooth. Serve over grilled meat.

Winthrop Rockefeller Institute Saturday Chef's Series

Desserts &
Other Sweets

Ozark Folk Center Fried Pies

3 ounces (just over ⅓ cup) evaporated milk
½ cup water
½ cup shortening, melted
1 ounce (2 tablespoons) white vinegar
2 cups self-rising flour
½ cup all-purpose flour
1 can pie filling (flavor of your choice)

Combine milk, water, shortening and vinegar. Add both flours. Using an electric mixer, mix until texture of dough is silky, not sticky or dry. Adjust with small amounts of liquid if too dry to roll or small amount of flour if sticky. Pull an amount the size of a big walnut and roll into ball. Roll this to a 6-inch circle on floured board or parchment paper. Place 4 ounces filling towards one side of circle. Brush edges of circle with evaporated milk. Fold in half and seal edges with fork or fingers. Punch holes in the top using a fork 2 times. This prevents explosion. Deep fry in vegetable oil at 350° for 5 minutes or until golden brown. Makes 12 pies.

Shirley Blackwell, Ozark Folk Center State Park

Possum Pie

2 (3-ounce) packages cream cheese, softened
¾ cup powdered sugar
1 (9-inch) graham cracker crust
¼ cup pecan pieces
⅓ cup instant chocolate pudding
2 cups milk
¾ teaspoon vanilla extract
½ cup whipping cream, whipped
12 to 16 pecan halves

In a mixing bowl, beat cream cheese and sugar until smooth. Spread onto bottom of the crust. Sprinkle with chopped pecan pieces. In another mixing bowl, combine pudding mix with milk and vanilla; beat on low speed 2 minutes. Spoon over pecans. Refrigerate at least 2 hours. Top with whipped cream and pecan halves. Makes 8 servings.

VW Festival, Swap Meet & Tourcade

All-American Strawberry Pie

¾ cup sugar
½ cup all-purpose flour
¼ teaspoon salt
3 cups milk
3 egg yolks, lightly beaten
2 tablespoons butter or margarine
1½ teaspoons vanilla extract
1 (9-inch) pie shell, baked
½ pint heavy cream
1½ tablespoons powdered sugar
1 pint fresh strawberries, halved
1 cup fresh or frozen blueberries

In a 3-quart saucepan, combine sugar, flour and salt. Add milk, stirring until smooth. Cook over medium heat, stirring, until thickened. Stir small amount of milk mixture into yolks; add to saucepan. Cook, stirring, for 2 minutes. Remove from heat; stir in butter and vanilla. Cool 20 minutes. Pour into pie shell; chill several hours until firm. Whip cream and powdered sugar; spread half over pie filling. Arrange berries on cream. Dollop or pipe remaining cream around edge of pie. Serves 8.

Festival on the Ridge
First weekend in June

Downtown Harrisburg
870.578.4104

The perfect way to kick off summer vacation is in downtown Harrisburg. Held the first Saturday in June, the Festival on the Ridge has everything needed for a day full of fun activities. The day begins with the annual 5K run. If running is not on the agenda, then head down to the country breakfast. When the race is over and the breakfast table cleared, it's time to show off your best horseshoe tossing technique in the popular Horseshoe Tournament. Does the nostalgia of a simpler time appeal to you? What better way to relive old memories and make new ones than with an old-fashioned Soap Box Derby! Hints of the past give way to live action extreme sports as the BMX Stunt Team shows off daring feats of skill. Speaking of skill, if you don't know the proper way to eat a mudbug, then the Crawfish Eating Contest is a must-see. Throughout the day, live music sets the tone for summer fun. For more information, contact the Harrisburg Area Chamber of Commerce at 870.578.4104.

No Fail Pecan Pie

⅓ cup butter
1 cup sugar
1 cup light corn syrup
4 eggs, beaten
1 teaspoon vanilla
¼ teaspoon salt
1 (9-inch) pie shell, unbaked
1 cup pecan halves

Combine butter, sugar and corn syrup in a medium saucepan. Cook over low heat, stirring constantly until sugar dissolves and butter melts. Cool slightly. Stir a small amount into beaten eggs (to prevent cooking eggs) then add beaten eggs into saucepan. Stir in vanilla and salt. Pour into unbaked pie shell and top with pecan halves. Bake at 325° for 50 minutes.

Magnolia Blossom Festival
& World Championship Steak Cook-Off®
Third Saturday in May

Downton Magnolia Square
Magnolia
870234-4352
blossomfestival.org

Are you a steak lover? Then the Magnolia Blossom Festival is the place for you! It is the home of the World Championship Steak Cook-Off®, and there you will find over 5000 16oz Angus Beef Ribeye steaks cooked to perfection. The fun begins with the Blossom Festival Parade, as each contestant makes their way down Main Street to the square to begin setting up for the competition.

Cherry Berry on a Cloud

Step 1 - Crust:
6 large egg whites
½ teaspoon cream of tartar
¼ teaspoon salt
1¾ cups sugar

In a large bowl beat egg whites, cream of tartar and salt until fluffy. Gradually beat in sugar until stiff. Spread in a buttered 9x13-inch glass baking dish, bringing some up the sides. Bake in a 275° preheated oven for 60 minutes. Turn off oven and leave crust in the oven for 12 hours (overnight).

Step 2 - Filling:
1 (8-ounce) package cream cheese, softened
1 cup sugar
1 teaspoon vanilla
1 large carton Cool Whip
1 cup sour cream
2 cups mini marshmallows

The next morning, mix cream cheese, sugar and vanilla. Gently fold in Cool Whip, sour cream and marshmallows. Spread over crust and refrigerate 8 hours or all day.

Step 3 - Topping:
1 can cherry pie filling
1 teaspoon lemon juice
½ teaspoon almond extract
1 small package sliced and drained strawberries

Mix topping ingredients and spread on top of filling. Refrigerate until topping is chilled and set.

Cammie Hambrice
Magnolia Chamber of Commerce
Magnolia Blossom Festival & World Championship Steak Cook-Off®

Dorothy's Mile-High Strawberry Pie

Crust:

1 cup flour
¼ cup brown sugar
½ cup nuts
¼ (1 stick) pound butter, melted

Filling:

1 (10-ounce) package frozen sliced strawberries, thawed
1 cup sugar
⅛ teaspoon salt
2 egg whites
1 teaspoon lemon juice
½ pint whipping cream or 1 envelope Dream Whip
1 teaspoon vanilla

Combine crust recipes. Spread ⅔ of mixture in a 9x13-inch pan; reserve the rest for crumb topping.   Bake pan 20 minutes at 350°. Stir 3 times while baking, so it will be a crumbly texture. Spread ⅔ of mixture in pan and save ⅓ for top. Cool completely. Place thawed strawberries in a large mixer bowl. Add sugar, salt, egg whites and lemon juice; beat 15 minutes on high speed until very thick. Whip cream until stiff; add vanilla. Fold the 2 mixtures together by hand. Pile in cooled crust (you can also use a 10-inch baked pie crust). Top with reserved crumb topping. Cover with foil and freeze.

Hot Springs Arts & Crafts Fair

Chiffon Lemonade Pie

1 can frozen lemonade
1 can Eagle Brand sweetened condensed milk
1 small carton Cool Whip
1 graham cracker crust

Combine all ingredients with electric mixer until well blended. Pour into crust and refrigerate at least 2 hours before serving.

Ruth Tate
BPW Barn Sale

Best Sugar Pie

2 cups brown sugar
1¼ cups all-purpose flour
½ cup heavy cream
1 egg
1 tablespoon corn syrup
1 teaspoon vanilla extract
¾ cup chopped pecans
1 (9-inch) unbaked pie crust

Preheat oven to 350°. In a medium bowl, mix together brown sugar and flour; set aside. In a large bowl, whisk together cream, egg, corn syrup and vanilla. Stir in brown sugar mixture until blended. Fold in pecans. Pour filling into pie crust. Bake in preheated oven for 30 to 40 minutes, or until golden brown.

Coconut Cream Pie

¼ cup cornstarch
⅔ cups sugar
1 can evaporated milk plus enough milk to make 3 cups
4 egg yolks
1 teaspoon vanilla
2 tablespoons butter, softened
1 cup coconut plus more for topping
1 (9-inch) pie shell, baked

Meringue:
3 egg whites
¼ teaspoon cream of tartar
6 tablespoons sugar
¼ cup flaked coconut

Combine all ingredients except butter and coconut in microwavable bowl. Cook in microwave 2 minutes; stir well. Repeat cooking and stirring until mixture thickens. Stir in butter and coconut. Pour into baked and cooled pie shell. For meringue, in a small mixing bowl, beat egg whites and cream of tartar on medium speed until soft peaks form. Gradually beat in sugar, 1 tablespoon at a time, on high until stiff glossy peaks form and sugar is dissolved. Spread evenly over filling, sealing edges to crust. Sprinkle with flaked coconut. Bake in 350° oven 30 minutes or until nicely browned.

Historic Oark General Store & Cafe

Apple Cranberry Crunch

3 cups coarsely chopped, unpeeled apples
2 cups fresh or frozen cranberries
¾ cup sugar

Topping:
½ cup old fashioned oats
¾ cup chopped pecans
½ cup dark brown sugar, packed
⅓ cup flour
1 stick butter, softened

Preheat oven to 350°. Combine s, cranberries and sugar in a medium bowl. Turn into a greased baking dish. (Deep dish pie pan works best.) Combine oats, pecans, brown sugar and flour. Stir in butter. Crumble over filling, press down lightly. Bake 45 minutes or until topping is brown and filling is bubbly.

Alice Chambers
Greers Ferry Lake/Little Red River Shoreline Cleanup

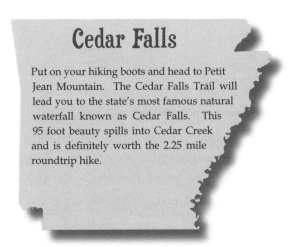

Cedar Falls

Put on your hiking boots and head to Petit Jean Mountain. The Cedar Falls Trail will lead you to the state's most famous natural waterfall known as Cedar Falls. This 95 foot beauty spills into Cedar Creek and is definitely worth the 2.25 mile roundtrip hike.

Company's Comin' Pie

Official state pie of Arkansas.

6 egg whites
1 teaspoon cream of tartar
2 cups sugar
1 teaspoon vanilla
1 sleeve saltine crackers, crushed
½ cup chopped pecans

Topping:
1 small container whipped topping
3 tablespoons sugar
2 tablespoons crushed pineapple

Beat egg whites until fluffy. Add cream of tartar and sugar. Beat 25 minutes or until stiff. Stir in vanilla. Stir in crackers and pecans by hand. Spray 2 pie pans with nonstick spray. Divide mixture evenly between pans. Spread mixture in pan forming a crust. Bake at 285° for 25 minutes or until done. Combine topping ingredients. Pour in to pie shell. Serve and enjoy.

The Cliff House Inn & Restaurant, Jasper
Buffalo River Elk Festival

Blue Ribbon Chocolate Chip Pie

2 eggs
½ cup all-purpose flour
½ cup sugar
½ cup firmly packed brown sugar
1 cup butter, melted and cooled to room temperature
1 (6-ounce) package semisweet chocolate chips
1 cup chopped pecans
1 (9-inch) pastry shell, unbaked
Whipped topping
Chocolate chips for garnish

Beat eggs until foamy. Add flour, sugar and brown sugar, beating until well blended. Add melted butter, chocolate and pecans. Pour filling into pastry shell. Bake at 325° for 1 hour or until filling is firm. Serve warm, topped with whipped topping and sprinkled with chocolate chips.

Thick, Chewy Chocolate Chip Cookies

1 cup (2 sticks) butter, softened
1½ cups firmly packed brown sugar
2 large eggs
1 teaspoon vanilla
2½ cups all-purpose flour
1 teaspoon baking soda
½ teaspoon salt
2 cups (12 ounces) semisweet chocolate chips
1 cup chopped pecans, optional

In a bowl, with an electric mixer on medium speed, beat butter and brown sugar until well blended. Beat in eggs and vanilla until smooth, scraping down sides of bowl as needed. In another bowl, mix flour, baking soda and salt. Stir or beat into butter mixture until well incorporated. Stir in chocolate chips and pecans. Drop dough in 2-tablespoon portions, 2 inches apart, onto buttered baking sheets. Bake in a 400° oven until cookies are lightly browned and no longer wet in the center (break one open to check), 6 to 8 minutes; if baking more than one pan at a time, switch pan positions halfway through baking. With a wide spatula, transfer cookies to racks to cool. If hot cookies start to break, slide a thin spatula under them to release; let stand on pan to firm up, 2 to 5 minutes, then transfer to racks to cool completely. Makes about 28 cookies

Oatmeal Lace Cookies

½ cup butter (real butter; margarine will not work), melted
1½ cups rolled oats
1 egg
⅔ cup sugar
1 teaspoon baking powder
1 tablespoon flour

Preheat oven to 350°. Combine butter and oats; set aside. In a separate bowl, beat egg until foamy. Add sugar and beat until light and fluffy. Stir in baking powder and flour. Fold in oat mixture. Grease and flour cookie sheets. Drop batter by tablespoons about 3 inches apart on cookie sheet. Bake until golden. Watch carefully; cookies will caramelize and burn easily. Cool cookies 1 minute then remove from sheets onto cooling racks. Cookies are very crispy and thin.

Mt. Magazine International Butterfly Festival

Mt. Magazine International Butterfly Festival
Weekend after Father's Day, June

Downtown Paris
479.963.2244
www.parisaronline.com

Lured by the many species of butterflies found on Mt. Magazine, enthusiasts gather annually on the weekend after Father's Day to participate in the Mt. Magazine International Butterfly Festival. Since 1997, thousands of people from 45 states and half a dozen countries have attended. Mt. Magazine has an extraordinary richness of butterfly species with virtually all Arkansas resident butterflies represented in good numbers in the State Park and valley below. The nation's showcase butterfly, and the Arkansas State Butterfly, the Diana fritillary (seen only occasionally in other parts of the U.S.), consistently reproduces on the mountain. The conjunctive festival occurs annually featuring events at the State Park and in the Gateway city of Paris (19 miles below the mountain). Events include arts, craft & food vendors, KIDZ Zone, Live Butterfly Conservatory, Art Show, Quilt Show, Photo Contest, Miss Butterfly Pageant and live entertainment. Check it out at www.butterflyfestival.com or www.ParisArOnline. com. Call the Paris Chamber for more information and exact dates 479.963.2244.

Flourless Peanut Butter Cookies

1 cup peanut butter
1 cup sugar
1 egg

Preheat oven to 350°. Combine ingredients and drop by teaspoonfuls onto an ungreased cookie sheet. Bake 8 minutes. Cool 1 to 2 minutes before removing to cooling racks.

Sharon Farmer
Diamond City Festival

Pat's Peanut Patties

2½ cups sugar
⅔ cup white Karo (corn) syrup
1 cup Pet (evaporated) milk
1½ cups raw peanuts
4 teaspoons butter
Red food coloring
1 cup powdered sugar

Combine sugar, syrup, milk and peanuts in a large saucepan. Cook slowly until it forms a good soft ball in cold water or at soft ball stage on a candy thermometer. Remove from heat. Add butter, a few drops of red food coloring and powdered sugar. Stir until mixture begins to thicken well. Drop by big spoonfuls onto wax paper or buttered cookie sheets. Allow plenty of room for spreading. Spread evenly. Cool before cutting into squares.

Pat Bailey
Diamond City Festival

Pecan Sandies

1 cup butter, softened
1 cup vegetable oil
1 cup sugar
1 cup powdered sugar
2 large eggs
1 teaspoon each vanilla extract, baking soda and cream of tartar
4 cups all-purpose flour
1 cup chopped pecans

Preheat oven to 350°. Combine butter and oil; add sugars. Blend well. Add eggs, vanilla, baking soda, and cream of tartar; blend. Slowly, cup-by-cup blend in flour and pecans. Chill 15 minutes. Form into balls and place by tablespoon full on cookie sheet sprayed with Pam. Cook 12 minutes. Remove from oven and cool on cookie rack. Makes about 4 to 5 dozen.

Tour da' Delta

Tour da' Delta
November

Helena
870.572.4147
www.tourdadelta.org

Winding through the Arkansas Delta every October / November is Tour da' Delta. The lake vistas, challenging hills, and a ride across the Mississippi River Bridge ensures this cycling adventure to be memorable indeed. Tour da' Delta is held in honor of the late Tom Kinnebrew, an avid cyclist and vigorous promoter of cycling in eastern Arkansas. Tom had planned much of the route before his passing, and his legacy lives on year after year. Bicyclists can choose from three different routes: 30 miles, 62 miles, and 100 miles. Along the way, rest stops are hosted and themed by a variety of local volunteers. At the conclusion of the ride, cyclists are treated with a BBQ feast and live music. Truly a community event, Tour da' Delta is a premier ride for all cyclists. Visit the website or call for the annual event dates, registration and other details.

Potato Chip Cookies

1 cup margarine, softened
¾ cup sugar
1 teaspoon vanilla
2 cups all-purpose flour
¾ cup crushed plain potato chips
½ cup chopped pecans

Cream margarine, sugar and vanilla until smooth. Add flour, chips and pecans and mix thoroughly by hand. Roll dough into balls, place on baking sheet and press with fork tines to flatten. Bake at 350° for 10 to 15 minutes. Makes 24 to 30.

Chocolate Raspberry Crumb Bars

1 cup margarine
2 cups flour
½ cup packed light brown sugar
¼ teaspoon salt
2 cups chocolate chips, divided
1¼ cups sweetened condensed milk
½ cup chopped nuts
⅓ cup seedless raspberry jam

Preheat oven to 350°. In large bowl, beat margarine till creamy. Beat in flour, sugar and salt till well mixed. Press 1¼ cup crumb mixture onto bottom of greased 9x13-inch baking dish. Reserve remaining crumb mixture. Bake 10 to 12 minutes, or till edges are golden brown. In a small saucepan, combine 1 cup chocolate chips and condensed milk. Melt over low heat, stirring, until blended. Spread over hot crust. Stir nuts into the reserved crumb mixture. Sprinkle over chocolate filling. Drop teaspoonfuls of raspberry jam over crumb mixture. Sprinkle with remaining chocolate chips. Continue baking 25 to 30 minutes or until center is set. Cool completely and cut into bars.

Wildflower Bed & Breakfast on the Square

Chocolate-Wine Balls

¼ cup honey
1 (6-ounce) package semi-sweet chocolate chips
2½ cups finely crushed vanilla wafer cookies (about 65 cookies)
2 cups walnuts
⅓ cup port sweet red wine or apple juice
½ cup coarse sugar crystals

Heat honey and chocolate chips in 3-quart saucepan over low heat, stirring constantly, until chocolate is melted; remove from heat. Stir in crushed cookies, walnuts and port. Shape into 1-inch balls; roll in sugar crystals. Store in a tightly covered container. Let stand several days to blend flavors. Flavor improves with age up to 4 weeks.

Eureka Springs Chocolate Lovers Festival

Eureka Springs Chocolate Lovers Festival
February

Best Western Inn of the Ozarks Convention Center
Eureka Springs
888.465.4753
www.eurekachocfest.com

A Valentine's Day extravaganza for the chocoholic in all of us—The Chocolate Lovers Festival is held every year, and it is the ultimate experience for the world's most delectable dessert. Come tantalize your taste buds where the fountains overflow with sumptuous chocolate. A complete world of chocolate delights waits for you—Rich dark chocolate, chocolate ice cream, chocolate drinks, chocolate body care products—there is something for everyone. Is baking with chocolate your specialty? Then be sure to enter the chocolate baking contest for professionals, amateurs and youth. The 1st and 2nd place winners are featured during the silent auction held during the festival. The Annual Chocolate Lovers Festival is held at the Inn of the Ozarks Convention Center. For more information, call 888.465.4753 or 479.253.7603 or visit our website at www.eurekachocfest.com or email: info@eurekachocfest.com. Admission: $10 adults, $6 for children 6 and under. All proceeds are presented to various charities.

Black Bottom Cupcakes

1 box chocolate cake mix, plus ingredients
    to prepare according to package directions
⅓ cup sugar
1 (8-ounce) package cream cheese, softened
1 egg
Dash salt
1 (6-ounce) package semisweet chocolate chips (1 cup)

Prepare cake mix according to package directions. Place paper baking cups in muffin pan; fill each one ⅔ full. Cream sugar and cream cheese; add egg and salt. Stir in chocolate pieces. Drop 1 rounded teaspoon into each cupcake. Bake per package directions. Delicious cream cheese filling makes it unnecessary to frost these fun cupcakes.

Simple Tea Cakes

2 eggs
⅔ cup cooking oil
¾ cup sugar
2 cups self-rising flour
1 teaspoon vanilla

Beat eggs well. Add oil and sugar, then flour and vanilla. Spray cookie sheet lightly with nonstick spray and drop dough by rounded spoonfuls. Bake at 300° until light brown, approximately 10 to 12 minutes.

Bright White Cake

This cake is wonderful and versatile. Try it with a different frosting each time it is made. Our family likes it hot out of the oven and topped with butter.

2 ¼ cups sifted cake flour
1 ½ cups sugar
3 ½ teaspoons baking powder
1 teaspoon salt
½ cup shortening
1 cup milk, divided
1 ½ teaspoons vanilla extract
4 egg whites

Preheat oven to 350°. Grease and flour 9x13-inch pan or 2 round cake pans. In a large bowl, mix flour, sugar, baking powder and salt. Add shortening, ¾ cup milk and vanilla. Beat until smooth. Add egg whites, unbeaten, and remaining milk. Beat about 2 minutes. Pour batter into pans. Bake round pans 30 to 35 minutes or 9x13-inch pan 35 to 40 minutes. Cool completely before removing and frost as desired.

Dump Cake

1 can crushed pineapple
1 can cherry pie filling
1 box dry yellow cake mix
1½ sticks butter
½ cup nuts

Frosting:
¾ cup sugar
1 (5½-ounce) can evaporated milk
1 stick butter

Preheat oven to 350°. In a 9x13-inch pan, dump crushed pineapple and spread it out. Dump in cherry pie filling and spread. Dump in cake mix and spread over fruit. Cut butter over top. Sprinkle with nuts. Bake 45 minutes to 1 hour, or until top is bubbly. About 15 minutes before cake is done, combine frosting ingredients in a saucepan over medium-high heat. Boil 10 minutes and pour immediately over hot cake.

Helen Largent
Diamond City Festival

Chopped Apple Cake

2 cups chopped apples
1½ cups sugar, divided
1 egg
½ cup Wesson oil
1½ cups flour
1 teaspoon soda
½ teaspoon salt
½ teaspoon cinnamon
¼ teaspoon nutmeg
1 cup chopped nuts
Juice of 1 lemon

Mix apples with 1 cup sugar; set aside for 10 minutes. Beat egg with oil. Add dry ingredients; mix well. Stir in nuts. Bake at 350° for 45 minutes. For glaze, bring ½ cup sugar and juice of 1 lemon to a boil. Pour over warm cake.

Elaine Scudder, Little Rock Farmers' Market
Jane and Elaine's Plants and Produce

Cinnamon Coffee Cake

Topping:
½ cup sugar
2 tablespoons cinnamon
½ cup pecans

Cake:
1 box Pillsbury yellow cake mix
1 box instant vanilla pudding
4 eggs
½ cup oil
1 cup sour cream

Combine topping ingredients and set aside. Combine cake ingredients with beater for 10 minutes. Pour small amount of batter in greased and floured tube pan. Sprinkle on a layer of topping. Do this three times ending with topping. Bake at 350° for 50 minutes.

Helen Sargent
Diamond City Festival

Ultimate Coffee Cake

16 to 18 unbaked frozen dinner rolls
1 (3-ounce) package butterscotch pudding mix (not instant)
½ cup packed brown sugar
½ cup chopped pecans
1 stick (½ cup) butter, melted

The night before, place frozen rolls in well-greased Bundt pan. Sprinkle dry pudding mix over rolls. Sprinkle brown sugar over pudding mix. Sprinkle chopped pecans over brown sugar. Pour melted butter over all. To prevent dough from forming a hard crust while its rising overnight, cover with a damp towel or tightly wrap with plastic wrap. Let rise overnight at room temperature, about 8 to 10 hours. Preheat oven to 350°. Bake 30 minutes. Remove from oven and allow to cool 5 minutes. Turn pan over onto a serving platter to remove. Serve by pulling apart chunks with forks.

Coke Cake

2 cups sugar
2 cups flour
1 teaspoon baking soda
2 tablespoons dry buttermilk
2 sticks butter
2 tablespoons cocoa
1 cup Coca Cola
½ cup water
2 eggs
1 teaspoon vanilla

Combine sugar, flour, soda and dry buttermilk in a mixing bowl. In a small saucepan, bring butter, cocoa, coke and water to a boil. Pour hot mixture over dry ingredients and beat well. Add eggs, one a time beating well after each. Add vanilla; batter will be thin. Pour into a 12x16-inch greased and floured cake pan. Bake 19 minutes in a 350° oven.

Icing:

1 stick butter
3 tablespoons cocoa
6 tablespoons Coca Cola
1 (16-ounce) box powdered sugar
1 teaspoon vanilla

Bring butter, cocoa, and coke to a boil in a small saucepan. Pour over powdered sugar. Add vanilla and beat well. Spread while still hot over hot cake.

Cammie Hambrice
Magnolia Chamber of Commerce
Magnolia Blossom Festival & World Championship Steak Cook-Off®

Milky Way Cake

4 (2.1-ounce) Milky Way candy bars
½ pound (2 sticks) butter, divided
2 cups sugar
4 large eggs
1 cup buttermilk
2½ cups unbleached flour, sifted
¼ teaspoon baking soda
2 teaspoons vanilla extract
1 cup coarsely chopped pecans

Melt Milky Ways and 1 stick butter in double boiler. Let cool. Preheat oven to 350°. Cream remaining 1 stick butter with sugar. Add eggs, beating after each. Add buttermilk alternately with flour and soda. Add vanilla and Milky Way mixture and mix until smooth. Fold in pecans. Pour into a greased and floured Bundt pan. Bake 1 hour or until cake tester comes out clean. Cool 15 minutes in the pan and then turn out on rack to finish cooling. Serve with scoops of ice cream on top of each slice for a taste delight. Serves 10.

Rock 'n Roll Highway 67 Music Festival

Chocolate Pound Cake

1 cup butter, softened
½ cup vegetable shortening
3 cups sugar
5 eggs
3 cups sifted all-purpose flour
½ teaspoon baking powder
½ teaspoon salt
¼ cup cocoa
1 cup milk
1 teaspoon vanilla

Preheat oven to 325°. Cream butter, shortening and sugar until smooth. Add eggs, 1 at a time, beating well after each addition. Sift flour, baking powder, salt and cocoa together. Alternately add dry ingredients and milk to creamed mixture. Stir in vanilla. Pour batter into greased and floured 10-inch tube pan. Bake 1 hour and 20 minutes or until toothpick inserted near center comes out clean.

Best Ever Brownie Cake

This cake is a hit at every family gathering. The key is the frosting.

1 cup butter
1 cup water
⅓ cup cocoa
2 cups all-purpose flour
2 cups sugar
1 teaspoon baking soda
½ teaspoon salt
2 eggs
½ cup sour cream

Preheat oven to 375°. Grease and flour a jelly roll pan or large sheet pan. Heat 1 cup butter, 1 cup water and ⅓ cup cocoa to boiling in saucepan, stirring occasionally. Remove from heat. Add flour, sugar, baking soda, salt, eggs and sour cream; beat until smooth. This makes a very thin batter. Pour into pan. Bake 20 to 25 minutes or until toothpick inserted in the center comes out clean. Cool completely.

Frosting:

½ cup butter
⅓ cup cocoa
⅓ cup milk
1 (16-ounce) package powdered sugar
1 teaspoon almond extract
Dash salt

Heat butter, cocoa and milk to boiling in saucepan, stirring occasionally. Remove from heat. Add powdered sugar and beat until smooth. Stir in almond extract and salt. Pour frosting over cooled cake.

Brownie Mix in a Jar

Makes the perfect gift for teachers, Sunday school teachers, new neighbors... anyone that needs a bit of chocolate joy.

1¼ cups all-purpose flour
1 teaspoon baking powder
1 teaspoon salt
⅔ cup unsweetened cocoa powder
2¼ cups sugar
½ cup chopped pecans

Combine flour, baking powder and salt; add to quart jar. Add a layer of cocoa, press down firmly, then wipe the inside of the jar so the other layers will show through the glass. Repeat layering sugar and pecans, one a time, press each down firmly before proceeding to next layer. Attach a tag with the following instructions: Preheat oven to 350°. Grease and flour a 9x13-inch baking pan. Empty brownie mix into a large mixing bowl, and stir to blend. Add ¾ cup melted butter and 4 eggs; mix well. Spread batter evenly into prepared baking pan. Bake 25 to 30 minutes. Cool completely in pan before cutting into 2-inch squares.

Brownie Trifle

1 (19.8-ounce) package fudge brownie mix,
  plus ingredients to prepare per package directions
Kahlua coffee liqueur
2 (3.9-ounce) packages chocolate fudge instant pudding mix,
  plus ingredients to prepare per package directions
8 Heath candy bars, coarsely crushed (plus more for garnish if desired)
1 (16-ounce) container Cool Whip

Prepare brownie mix according to package directions in a 9x13-inch pan. (I put in 3 eggs for a more cake-like brownie.) Prick top of warm brownies at 1-inch intervals with a wooden toothpick and brush with coffee liqueur; cool. Prepare pudding according to directions, omit chilling. Crumble ½ brownies in a 3-quart trifle bowl. Top with ½ pudding, ½ crushed candy bars and ½ Cool Whip. Repeat with remaining brownies, pudding and topping. Cover and chill 8 hours or overnight. Garnish with additional crushed candy bars, if desired.

Nita Pilkington, Sherwood
Christmas Trail of Lights

Christmas Trail of Lights
First week of December through December 30, nightly

City of Sherwood
501.835.5319

In 2001, the city of Sherwood began providing its holiday trail of lights to the community. This free, mile long, driving trail through holiday lights provides 90+ lit displays ranging from traditional Christmas displays (Santa Claus and poinsettias) to the unique (reindeer in a

soda shop and Sherwood express train). Each passenger in the car receives a candy cane to enjoy while taking in the view of the holiday lights. Each year the success grows, 2010 marked the best year yet with number of cars and contributions. Money collected from the trail gets put back into the budget for the next year, making it bigger and better. Individuals and businesses are represented throughout the trail by either donating light displays or donating money to represent a memorial angel. The trail opens every year the first week in December and runs until December 30th, nightly. Sherwood is also host to several other community events including an Easter Egg Hunt, July 4th Celebration, Sherwood Fest and the Halloween Carnival. For more information regarding all Sherwood events please call 501.835.5319.

Chocolate Lava Muffins

1 (8-ounce) package semisweet chocolate chips
1 stick butter
½ teaspoon vanilla
½ cup sugar
3 tablespoons flour
¼ teaspoon salt
4 eggs

Melt chocolate, butter and vanilla together in a double boiler. In a separate bowl, mix together sugar, flour and salt. Sift dry ingredients into chocolate mixture; mix well. Add eggs one at a time, mixing well between each addition. Beat an additional 4 minutes. Chill batter 30 minutes to 1 hour. Line a muffin tin with foil cupcake liners. Fill each cup with 4 ounces batter. Bake at 375° for 7 to 10 minutes until sides are firm but middle is still soft. (Bake times may vary.) Makes 10 muffins. Serve with vanilla ice cream.

Heath & Natalie Dake, owners,
Foggy Hollow Cabin, Jasper
Cabins in the Ozarks

Lemon Bars

Bottom Layer:
2 sticks margarine, softened
2 cups flour
¼ cup sugar

Combine all ingredients. Press into 9x12-inch pan. Bake at 350° for 20 minutes.

Top Layer:
4 eggs
4 tablespoons flour
7 tablespoons lemon juice
2 cups sugar
½ teaspoon baking powder

Combine all ingredients. Pour over bottom layer. Return to oven and bake 20 minutes more. Bars will remain gooey in the center. Remove from oven and sprinkle with powdered sugar.

Cheryl Guthrie
Diamond City Festival

Arkansas Railroad Museum

1700 Port Road • Pine Bluff • 870.535.8819

Visit the home of Engine 819, Pine Bluff's legendary queen of steam, weighing in at 368 tons and measuring 100 feet from front to back. The museum also houses passenger cars, cabooses and baggage cars, all restored to their original splendor; as well as many artifacts used back in the days of steam engines.

— Pine Bluff Convention
& Visitors Bureaus

Leche Flan (Philippines)

1 cup plus 2 tablespoons sugar, divided
2 eggs, separated
6 egg yolks
1 can condensed milk
1 cup milk
2 tablespoons sugar
Zest of 1 lime

Caramelize sugar by continually stirring over medium heat until melted. Pour into flan mold (or any 8- or 9-inch glass oven ware). Tilt to completely coat bottom of mold. Beat egg yolks. In a separate bow, beat egg whites slightly. Combine yolks and whites with condensed milk, milk, sugar and lime zest. Strain and pour over caramel in mold. Place mold in another bigger sauce pan (bain marie); fill with water to about 1 inch from bottom. Bring to a boil and simmer 30 minutes or until set (insert toothpick to be sure). Cool completely before removing.

Asian Festival

Asian Festival
June

Mosaic Church
Little Rock
501.244.2490
www.arasianfestival.com

The Asian Festival is a celebration of the Asian culture and the diversity of the Little Rock community. The Asian Festival was established to encourage friendship and reduce prejudice by coming together to learn about different cultures and ethnicities. One of the goals of the festival through this annual event is to celebrate the global fabric of the City's social diversity. This is accomplished through the enjoyment of a variety of local performers, cultural exhibits, traditional music, dance, different ethnic foods, art, literature and silent auction, retailers, business information, health and wellness will be on hand. Of course, the children are not forgotten! Kids game area, hula hoop contest, jump rope and bouncy castle. Play many of the games and win prizes! Sponsors and local businesses donate fabulous auction items and door prizes are given every hour. The Asian Festival is held every year in June. Visit our website for dates and schedules. We look forward to seeing you there.

Baked Peanut Chocolate Mousse

12 peanut sable cookies (or Oreos, crushed)
8 ounces semi-sweet chocolate, chopped
8 ounces bitter-sweet chocolate, chopped
1 cup crunchy peanut butter
3 ounces butter
1 cup heavy cream
6 eggs, room temperature
½ cup sugar
½ teaspoon salt

Preheat oven to 325°. Line 12 (3- to 4-inch) ramekins or ring molds (or one 9- to 10-inch springform pan) with parchment paper on the bottom and around sides (cut parchment so that it is taller than the sides of the molds). Wrap bottoms of ring molds or springform pan with plastic wrap and then again with aluminum foil as a precaution against water leaking in. Place a peanut sable cookie round on the bottom of each ramekin (or cover bottom with Oreo crumbs). Melt chocolates, peanut butter and butter in a bowl over (but not touching) a pot of simmering water. Keep warm. Whip the cream in a small mixer until stiff peaks form. Set aside. Whip eggs, sugar, and salt in an upright mixer on high speed until tripled in volume (about 8 minutes). The eggs will triple in size and look like soft whipped cream. Fold melted chocolate into whipped eggs. Gently fold in cream.

Divide evenly into each ramekin, mold or springform pan. Place into a pan with sides and fill ¼ of the way with water (a 9x14-inch pan works well). Bake about 25 to 30 minutes (almost an hour if using the springform pan). The tops will look dry like a brownie and will puff slightly. Cool in pan about 10 minutes. Remove and cool in the refrigerator. When fully cooled, remove plastic wrap and foil. To remove from molds, heat them slightly (less than 3 minutes in an oven); they should pop out. You can use the tip of a paring knife to gently loosen the bottom. Remove parchment and serve with whipped cream and chocolate sauce. For the springform pan, cut it with a hot knife. This will keep several days in the refrigerator. Serve at room temperature.

Bella Vista Arts & Crafts Festival

Elms Delicious No Fail Fudge

1 (16-ounce) bag butterscotch chips
2 (16-ounce) bags semi-sweet or milk chocolate chips
1 can Eagle brand milk
1½ cups chopped pecans

Microwave all ingredients, except pecans, for 1 minute; stir.
Repeat until blended, but watch closely (do not overcook).
Add pecans. Pour into buttered Pyrex dish. Let stand several
hours. Makes 2 dozen pieces.

The Elms Plantation

The Elms Plantation

870.766.8337 • *www.theelmsplantation.com*

Displaying an elegant and colorful past in an atmosphere true to the Old South, The Elms Plantation provides a variety of facilities ranging from private suites and cottages to a special events center. "Whether you want a quiet weekend, an extended stay, or an afternoon visit for a rich, classic southern dessert, The Elms Plantation has accommodations that are right for you," owner, Kim Freeman said.

The Elms offers a English-Louisiana raised cottage style architecture along with prominent historical details including original glass paned windows and solid walnut staircases. You will find more than 140 years of Southern tradition, history, and luxury at the Elms.

Lavender Chocolate Fudge

⅔ cup evaporated milk
1 tablespoon dried lavender (use less, if desired)
1½ cups sugar
2 tablespoons butter or margarine
¼ teaspoon salt
2 cups miniature marshmallows
1½ cups semisweet chocolate chips
1 teaspoon vanilla

Line an 8-inch square baking pan with foil. Pour evaporated milk and lavender in medium, microwave-safe bowl. Microwave on high for 1 minute. Cover with plastic wrap and set aside to steep for 10 minutes. Strain into medium, heavy-duty saucepan; discard lavender. Add sugar, butter and salt to saucepan; bring to a full rolling boil over medium heat, stirring constantly. Boil, stirring constantly, for 4 to 5 minutes. Remove from heat. Add marshmallows; stir vigorously until almost melted. Stir in chocolate chips and vanilla until melted. Pour into prepared baking pan; refrigerate 2 hours or until firm. Lift from pan; remove foil. Cut into 48 pieces.

Eureka Springs Chocolate Lovers Festival

Bread Pudding with Sorghum Sauce

½ cup light brown sugar
½ cup sugar
2 eggs
2 cups milk
¼ cup melted butter
1 package crescent rolls, baked per directions and torn into pieces.

Combine all Bread Pudding ingredients, pour into dish and bake at 400° for 45 minutes.

Sorghum Sauce:

½ cup light brown sugar
1 tablespoon sorghum
1 tablespoon Karo (white corn) syrup
¼ cup butter
½ cup heavy cream
1 teaspoon vanilla

Combine all ingredients in saucepan over medium heat. Bring to a boil, stirring frequently. Reduce to medium low and boil 5 minutes. Remove from heat. Sauce will thicken as it cools. When cool, pour over cooled Bread Pudding.

Parker Homestead Festival

Bread Pudding

8 regular hamburger buns
8 eggs
2½ cups sugar
1 cup melted butter
4 cups milk

2 tablespoons pure vanilla
Cinnamon
Sugar in the Raw
Pecans, optional

Sauce:

1 (14-ounce) can sweetened condensed milk
¼ cup butter

¼ to ½ cup vanilla rum (or different liquor)
1 teaspoon vanilla extract

Pinch hamburger buns in to pieces and place in a greased 9x13-inch casserole dish. Combine eggs, 2½ cups sugar, butter, milk (if you really want to be bad, use half and half) and vanilla in a separate bowl. Pour over bread. Sprinkle with cinnamon and Sugar in the Raw to taste. Sprinkle pecans over the top, if you like. Bake in preheated 350° oven 45 minutes or until set. Cook sweetened condensed milk and butter in a saucepan over LOW heat until butter melts. Remove from heat; stir in rum and vanilla. Pour over hot bread pudding.

King Biscuit Blues Festival

King Biscuit Blues Festival
Columbus Day Weekend in October

Historic Downtown Cherry Street
Helena-West Helena
870.572.5223
www.kingbiscuitfestival.com

On a mission to sustain the culture, the heritage, and the authenticity of Delta Blues, the King Biscuit Blues Festival is held every Columbus Day Weekend in October on the banks of the Mississippi River. Tens of thousands of blues enthusiasts, as well as historians, from all over the world converge upon Historic Downtown Helena, Arkansas to hear stirring and uplifting performances of this American art form. The King Biscuit Blues Festival is one of the nation's foremost showcases of Blues Music. King Biscuit Blues Festival had its beginning in 1986, and was named after King Biscuit Time radio program, the longest running Blues radio program in the country. King Biscuit Time began in 1941 and still airs each week day at 12:15 on KFFA Radio in Helena, Arkansas.

Fall Harvest Pumpkin Treats

2 cups all-purpose flour
1 cup oats
1 teaspoon baking soda
1 teaspoon cinnamon
½ teaspoon salt
¾ cup butter
1 cup firmly packed brown sugar
½ cup sugar
1 egg
½ teaspoon vanilla
1 cup canned pumpkin pureé
1 cup raisins
½ cup chopped walnuts (optional)

Preheat oven to 350°. Grease cookie sheet. In a large bowl, combine flour, oats, baking soda, cinnamon and salt. In a separate bowl, cream butter and sugars until smooth. Add ½ cup of flour mixture and ¼ cup pumpkin. Stir. Repeat until all the flour and puree have been added. Stir in the raisins and nuts until blended. Drop by the tablespoons onto a greased cookie sheet 1 inch apart. Bake 12 to 15 minutes or until golden.

Index

Index of Events & Places

This Index is meant to be a tool for locating all events and places featured in *Eat & Explore Arkansas*. Each event or place is listed by both name and city referencing the page number for its featured page. Events and places that have a recipe are additionally listed by event or place name then recipe, referencing the page number for the recipe. A complete Index of Recipes begins on page 180.

Index of Recipes

C

D

Map of Events & Places

How well did we explore Arkansas? This map showcases all the hotspots highlighted throughout the book. As you can see, we did our homework! Each region of Arkansas is represented, giving travelers and revelers a chance to hear music, buy original artists' creations, mine for quartz, or take in quirky roadside attractions, wherever they may be.

Arkansas is vast, so jump in your car and hit the road. Outdoor celebrations and events are represented on the map by a car. Something will be needed to carry souvenirs from place to place, so every town, bed and breakfast, and unique store is represented by a suitcase. The southern climate is mild and usually sunny, so sunglasses are a must! Each pair of shades marks historic points of interest, landmarks, natural wonders and other destinations we stumbled upon. North, South, East, West… The Delta, the mountains, vineyards, lakes and rivers… Counties and cities… We explored it all… in Arkansas!

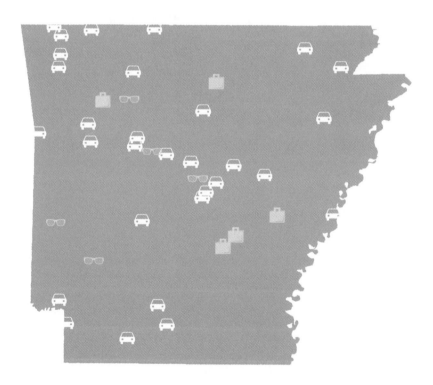

State Hometown Cookbook Series
A Hometown Taste of America, One State at a Time
EACH: $18.95 • 240 to 256 pages • 8x9 • paperbound

The STATE HOMETOWN COOKBOOK SERIES captures each state's hometown charm by combining great-tasting local recipes from real hometown cooks with interesting stories and photos from festivals all over the state. As a souvenir, gift, or collector's item, this unique series is sure to take you back to your hometown... or take you on a journey to explore other hometowns across the country.

Georgia Hometown Cookbook
978-1-934817-01-8 (1-934817-01-5)

Louisiana Hometown Cookbook
978-1-934817-07-0 (1-934817-07-4)

Tennessee Hometown Cookbook
978-0-9779053-2-4 (0-9779053-2-2)

Texas Hometown Cookbook
978-1-934817-04-9 (1-934817-04-X)

Mississippi Hometown Cookbook
978-1-934817-08-7 (1-934817-08-2)

• Easy to follow recipes produce great-tasting dishes every time.

• Recipes use ingredients you probably already have in your pantry.

• Fun-to-read sidebars feature food-related festivals across the state.

• The Perfect gift for anyone who loves to cook.

• Makes a great souvenir.

Collect Them All...
Eat & Explore Arkansas is the first book in the EAT AND EXPLORE STATE COOKBOOK SERIES. Call us toll-free 1.888.854.5954 to order additional copies or to be included in our Cookbook Club so you'll be notified of each new addition.

Coming Soon...
Eat & Explore Oklahoma

by Harold Webster
$16.95 • 240 pp • 7 x 10
paperbound • 978-0-9779053-1-7

292 Recipes for 30 Varieties of Wild Game

Respected hunter and chef Harold Webster shares 300 of his personal favorite recipes in his latest cookbook. As readers have come to expect, Webster's recipes are so easy to use that even a novice cook will be at home in kitchen yet interesting enough challenge the most experienced chef. In addition to the recipes, Webster tells fascinating stories about the capturing, cleaning and cooking of the game. Making this book an entertaining read as well as an essential resource for creating memorable meals from any hunter's Bounty.

Also Available from Great American Publishers:

900 recipes make up this outstanding collection created with the everyday cook in mind. Each cookbook features 150 easy-to-prepare recipes using common ingredients that are easily found in your local grocery store (most will already be in your kitchen).

EACH: $12.95 • 160 pp • 7x7½ • lay-flat paperbound

Quick Crockery Cooking • ISBN 978-0-9779053-3-1
Quick Desserts • ISBN 978-0-9779053-4-8
Quick Hors d'oeuvres • ISBN 978-0-9779053-5-5
Quick Mexican Cooking • ISBN 978-0-9779053-0-0
Quick Lunches & Brunches • ISBN 978-0-9779053-6-2
Quick Soups & Salads • ISBN 978-0-9779053-7-9

Order Form Mail to: Great American Publishers • P.O. Box 1305 • Kosciusko, MS 39090
Or call us toll-free 1888.854.5954 to order by check or credit card

❏ Check Enclosed

Charge to: ❏ Visa ❏ MC ❏ AmEx ❏ Disc

Card # _____

Exp Date _____ Signature _____

Name _____

Address _____

City _____ State _____ Zip _____

Phone _____

Email _____

QTY.	Title	Total
		Subtotal
Postage (3$ first book; $0.50 each additional)		
		Total